Doodle Book

Art Journal

Creative Kids

2014 ©

Date ....

Date……………………………………

Date ....

Date ....

Date ....

Date ....

Date..................................

Date ....

Date ....

Date ....

Date..................................

Date ....

Date ....

Date ....

Date ....

Date ....

Date...................................

Date ....

Date ……………………………………

Date..................................

Date ....

Date ....

Date ....

Date ....

Date …………………………………………

Date ....

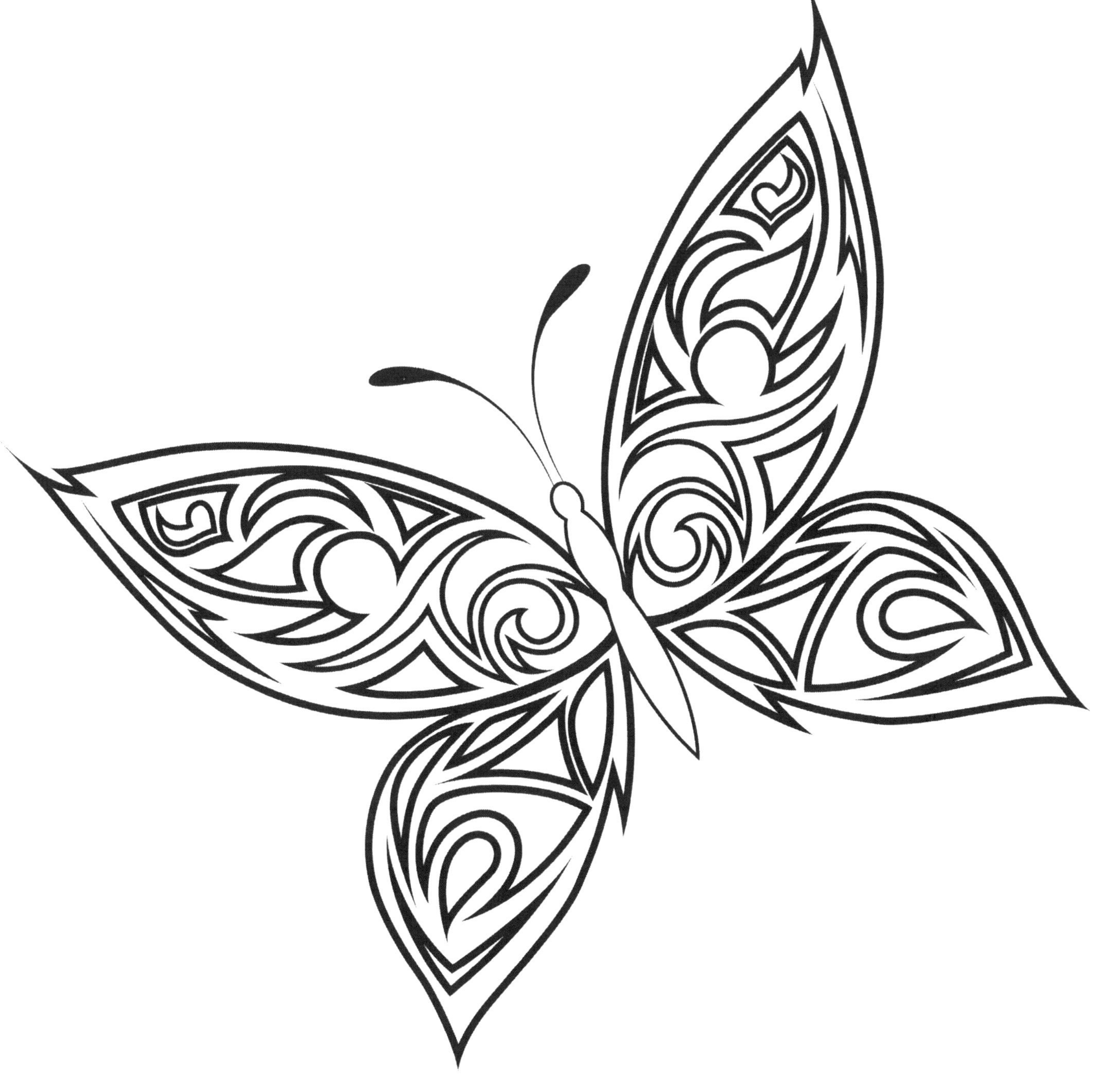

Date..................................

Date ....

Date..................................

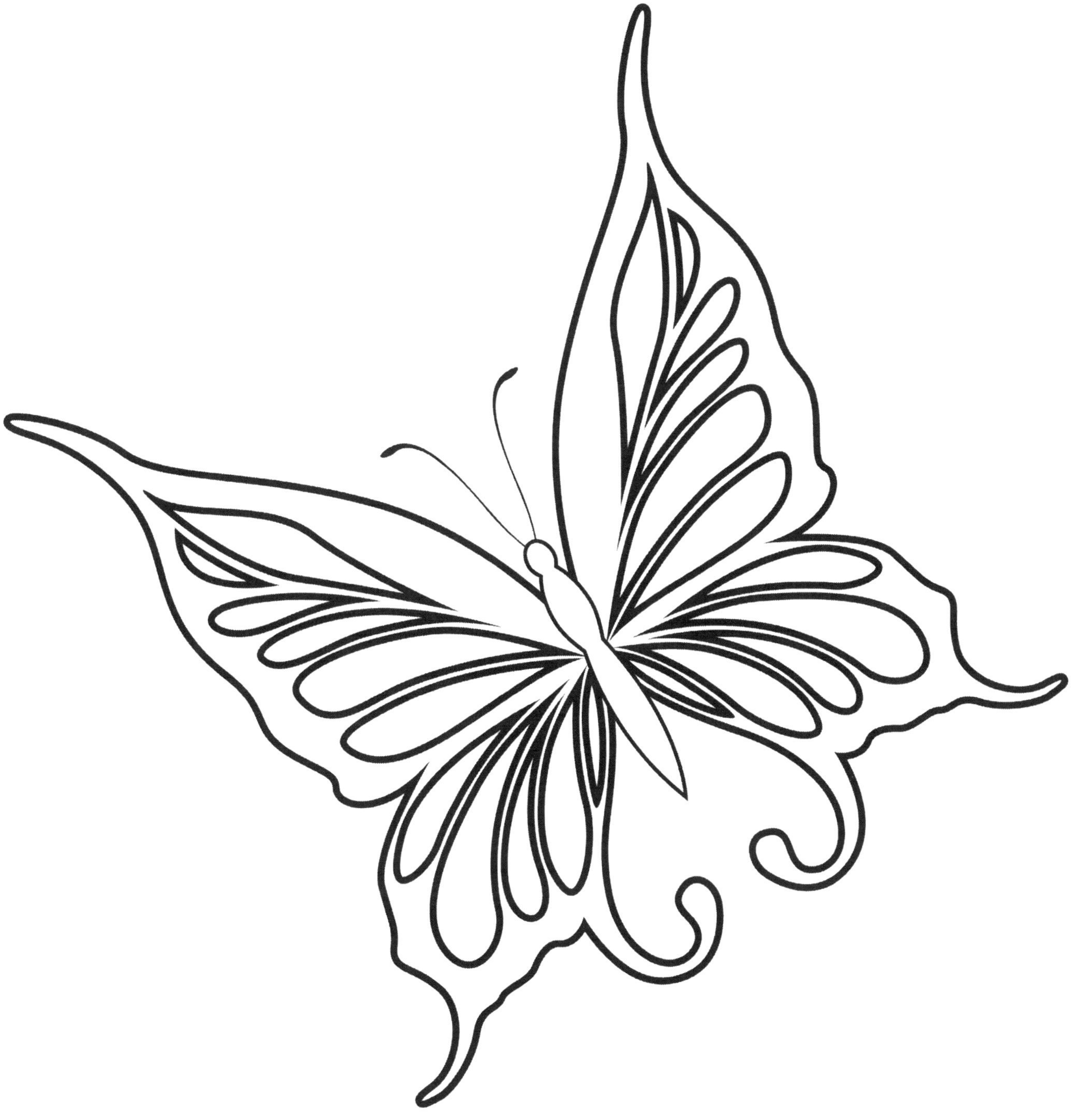

Date..................................

Date ....

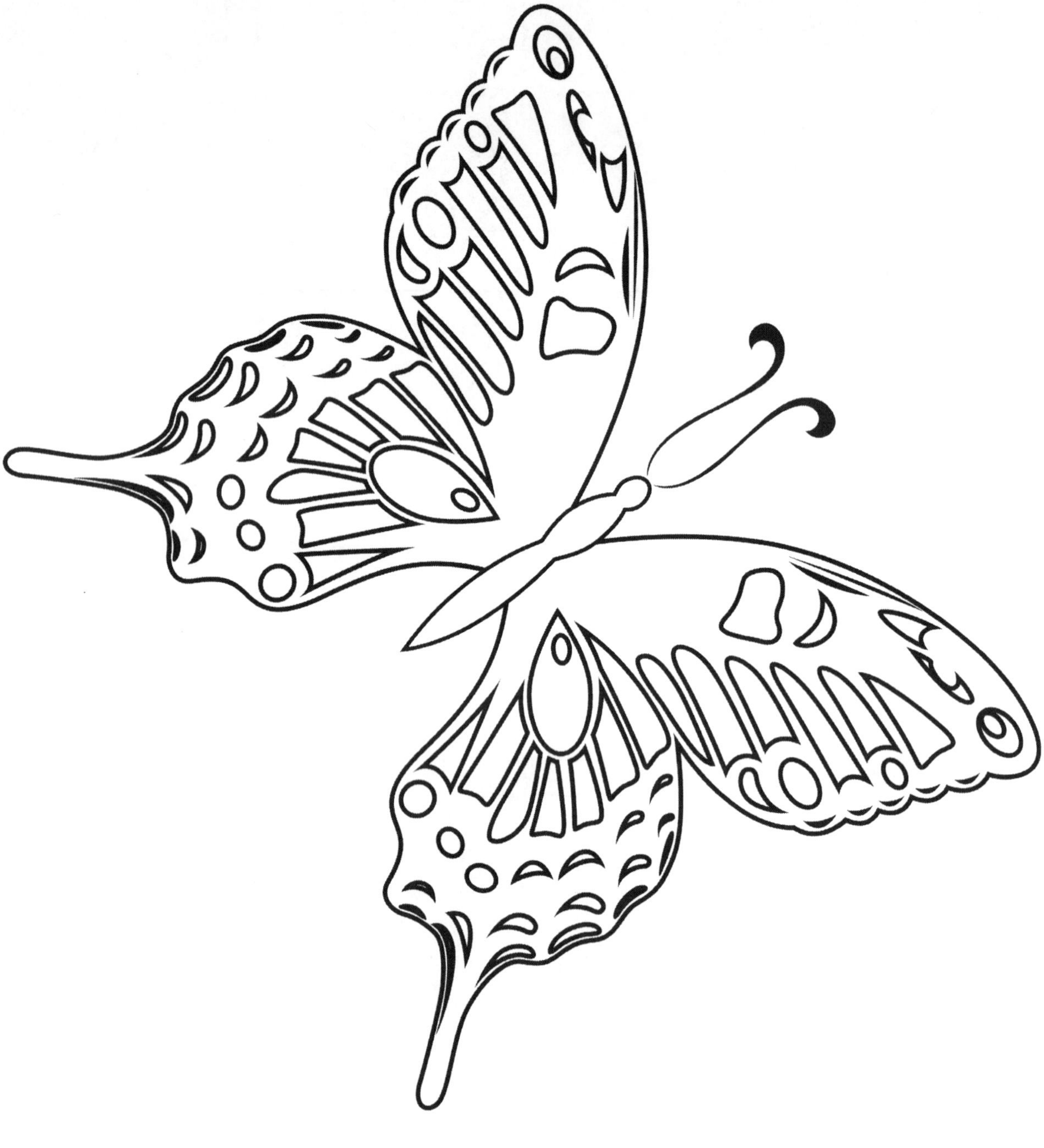

Date ....

Date ....

Date ....

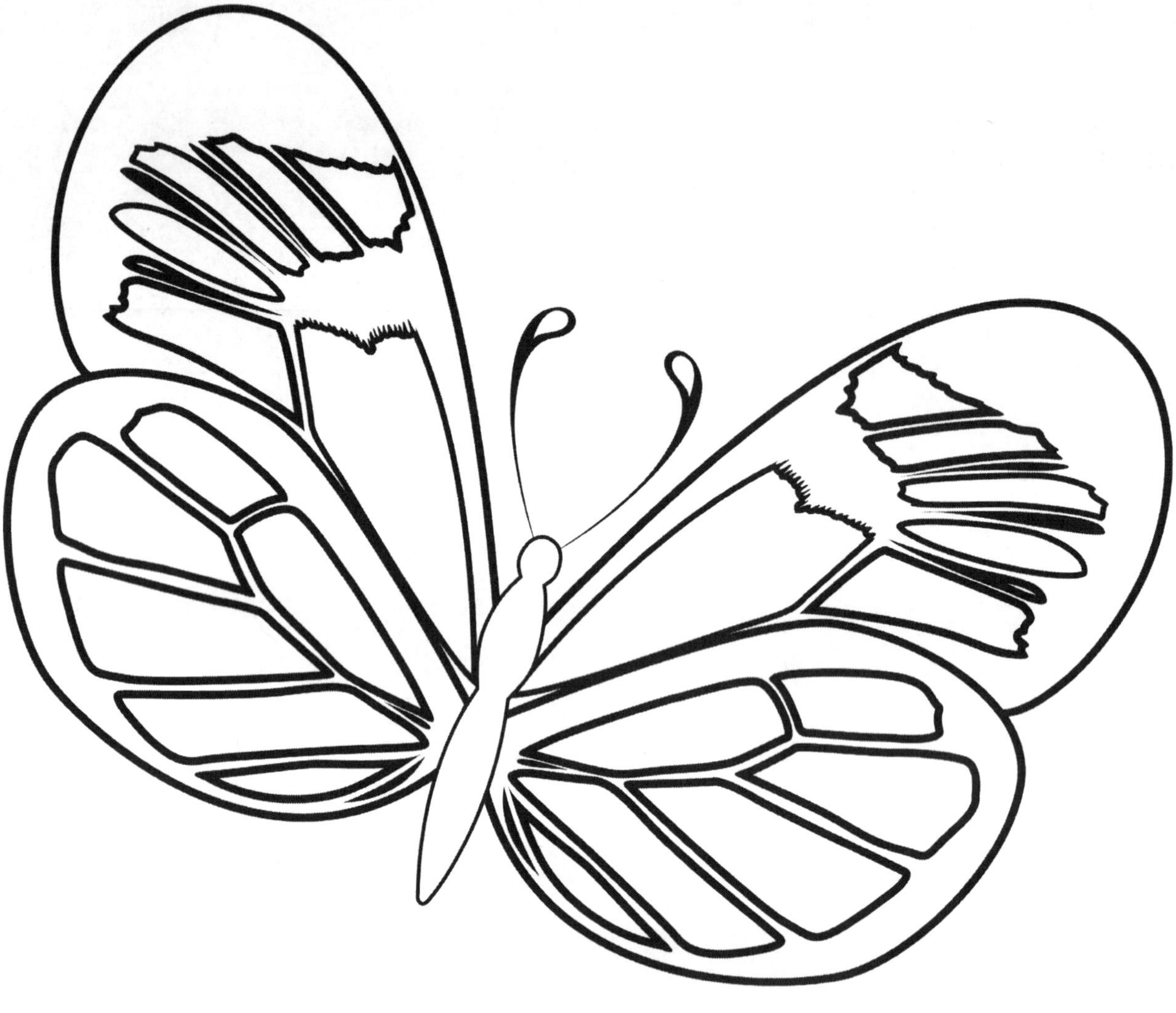

Date ....

Date……………………………………

Date …………………………………………

Date ....

Date ....

Date ....

Date……………………………..

Date ……………………………

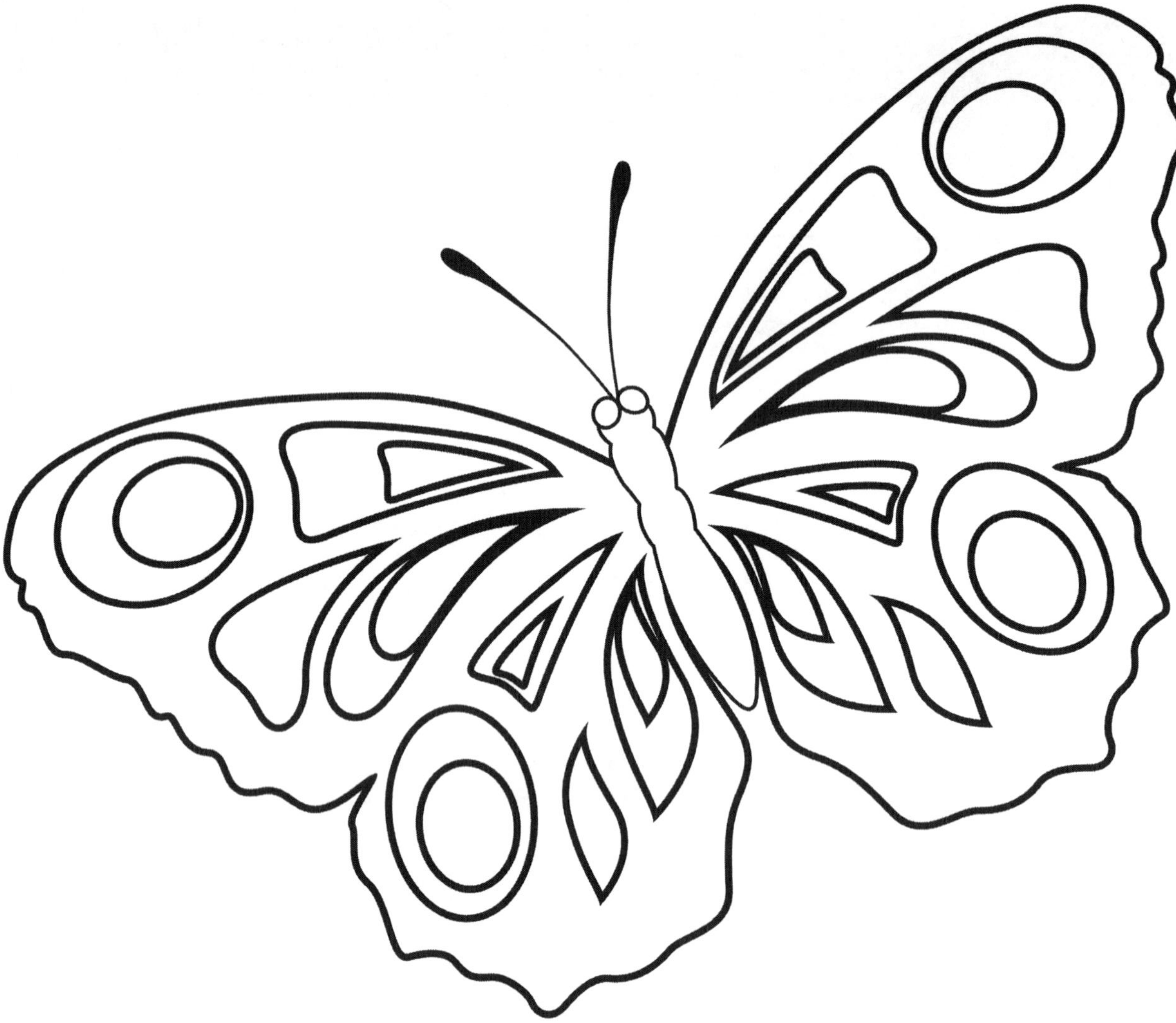

Date ....

Date ....

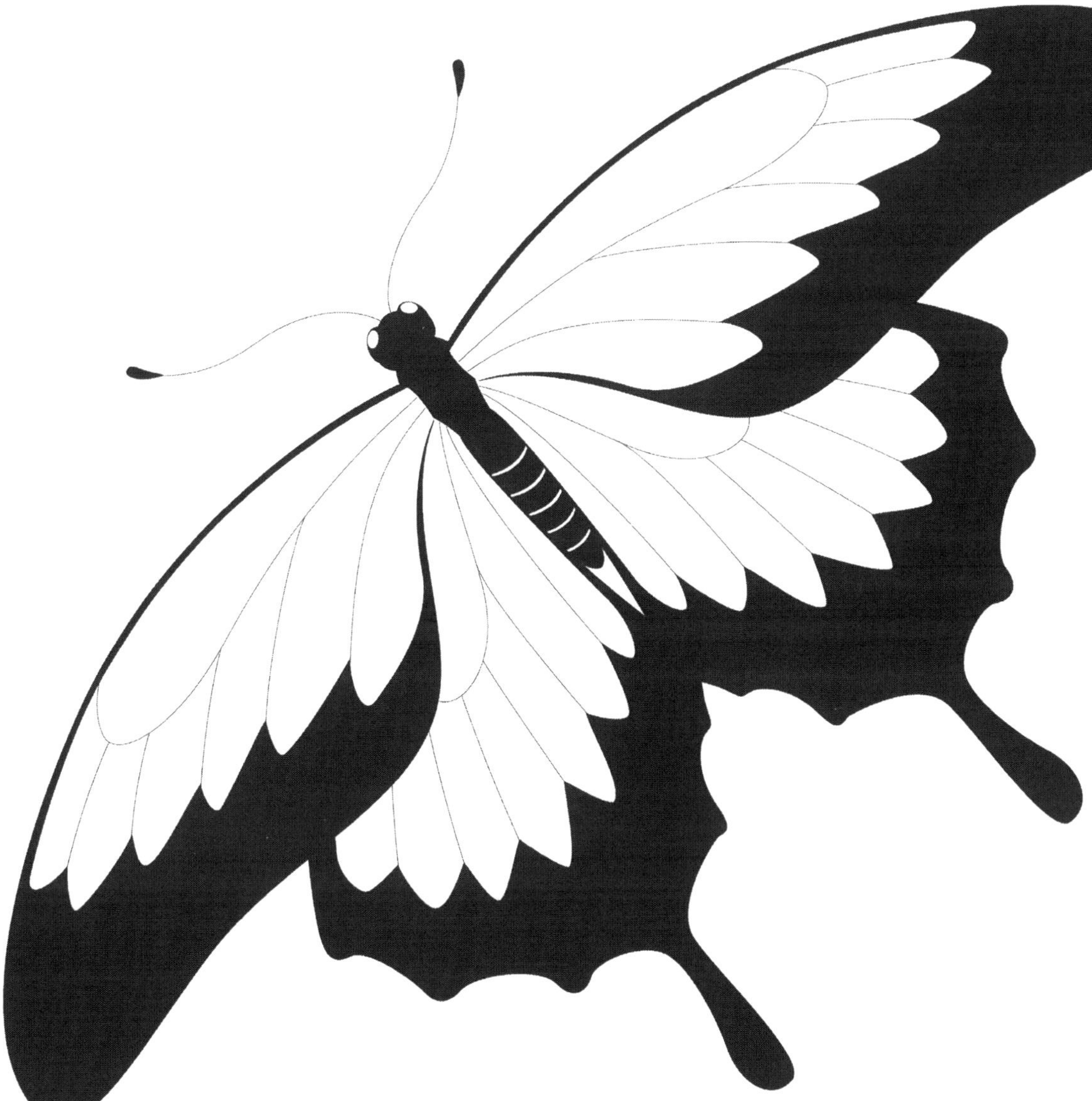

Date ....

Date ....

Date ....

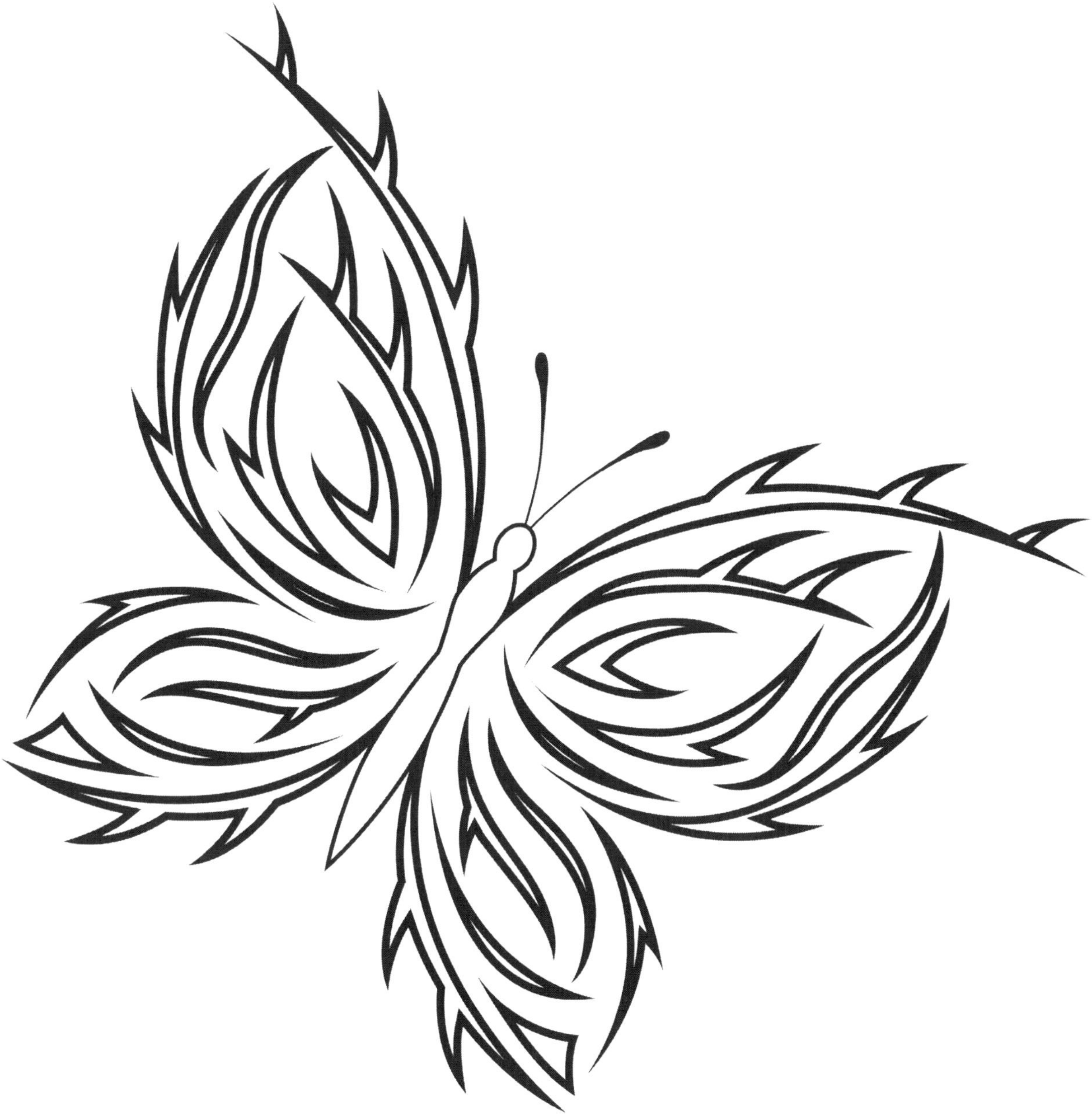

Date ....

Date ……………………………….

Date ....

Date ....

Date ....

Date ....

Date ....

Date ....

Date ....

Date ....

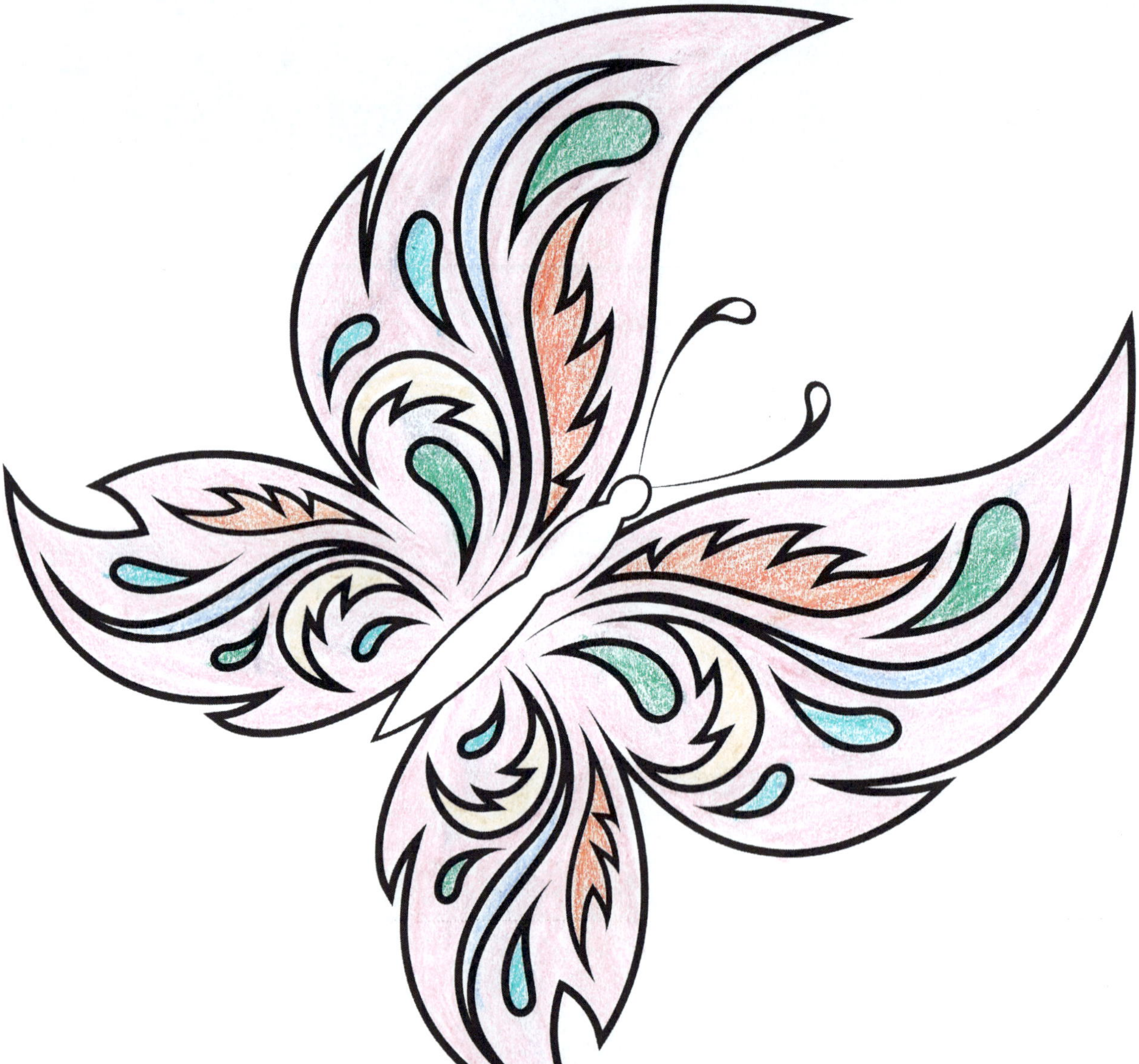

Date ....

Date ....

Date ....

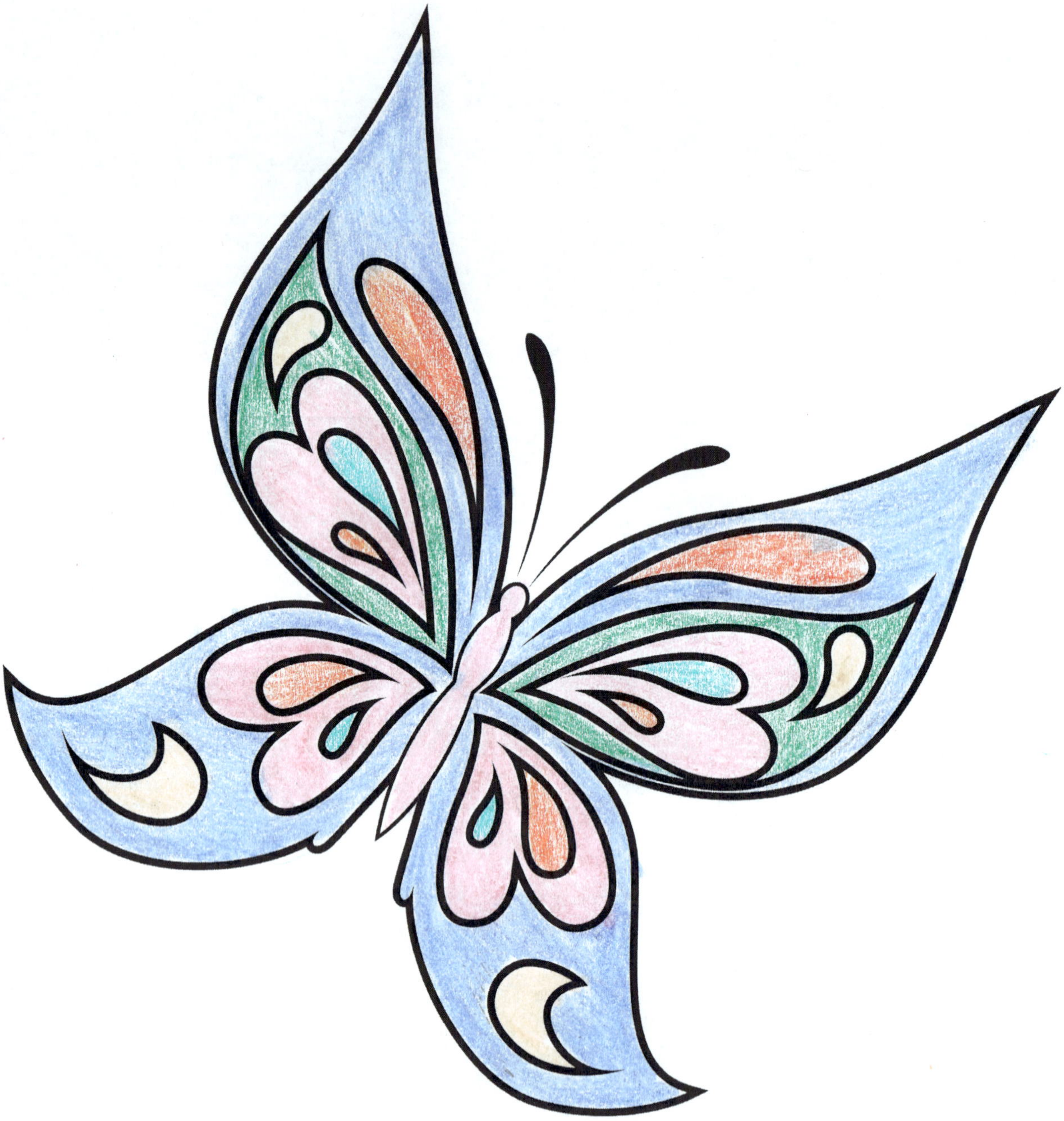

Date ....

Date ....

Date ....

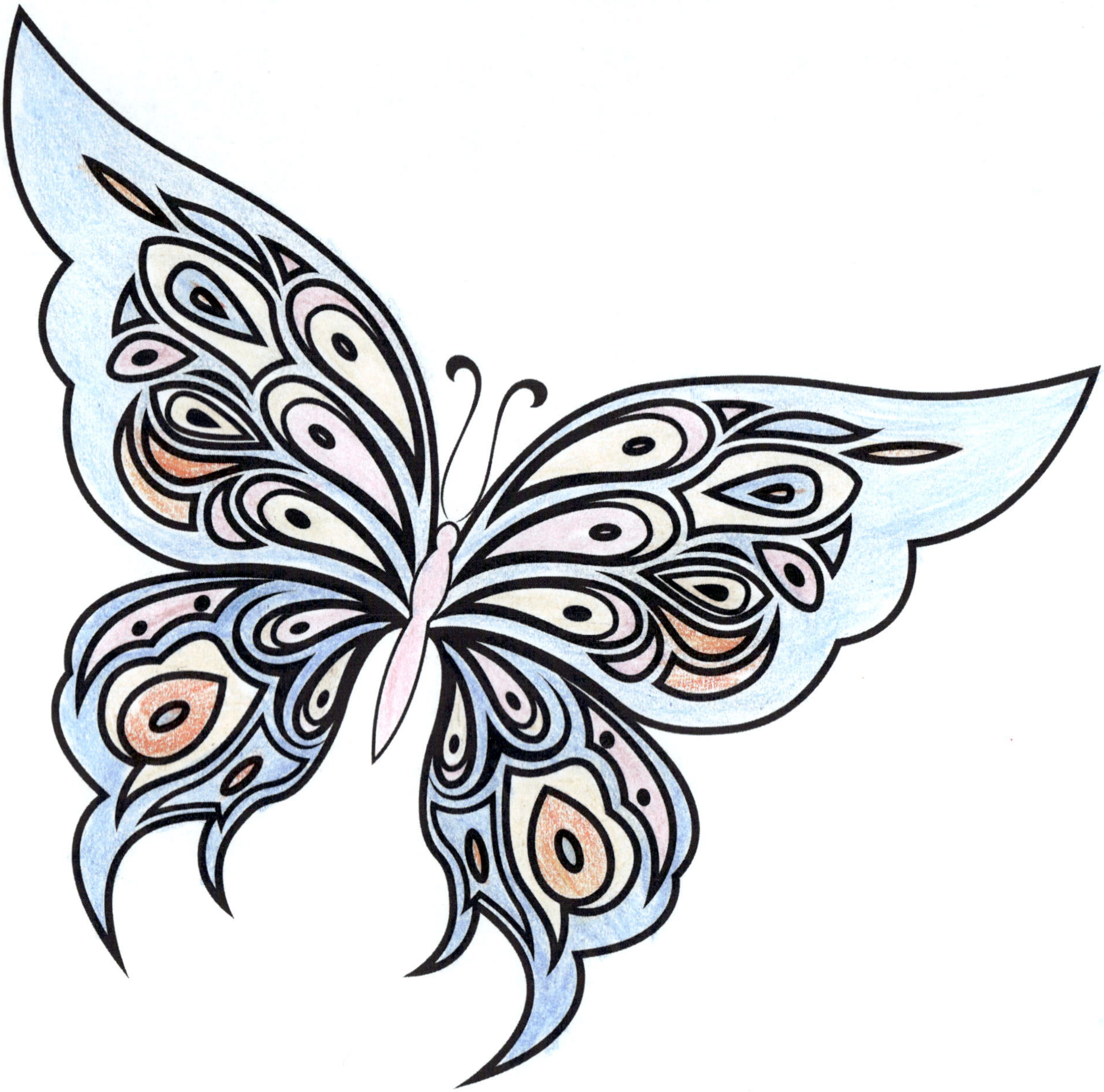

Date ....

Date ....

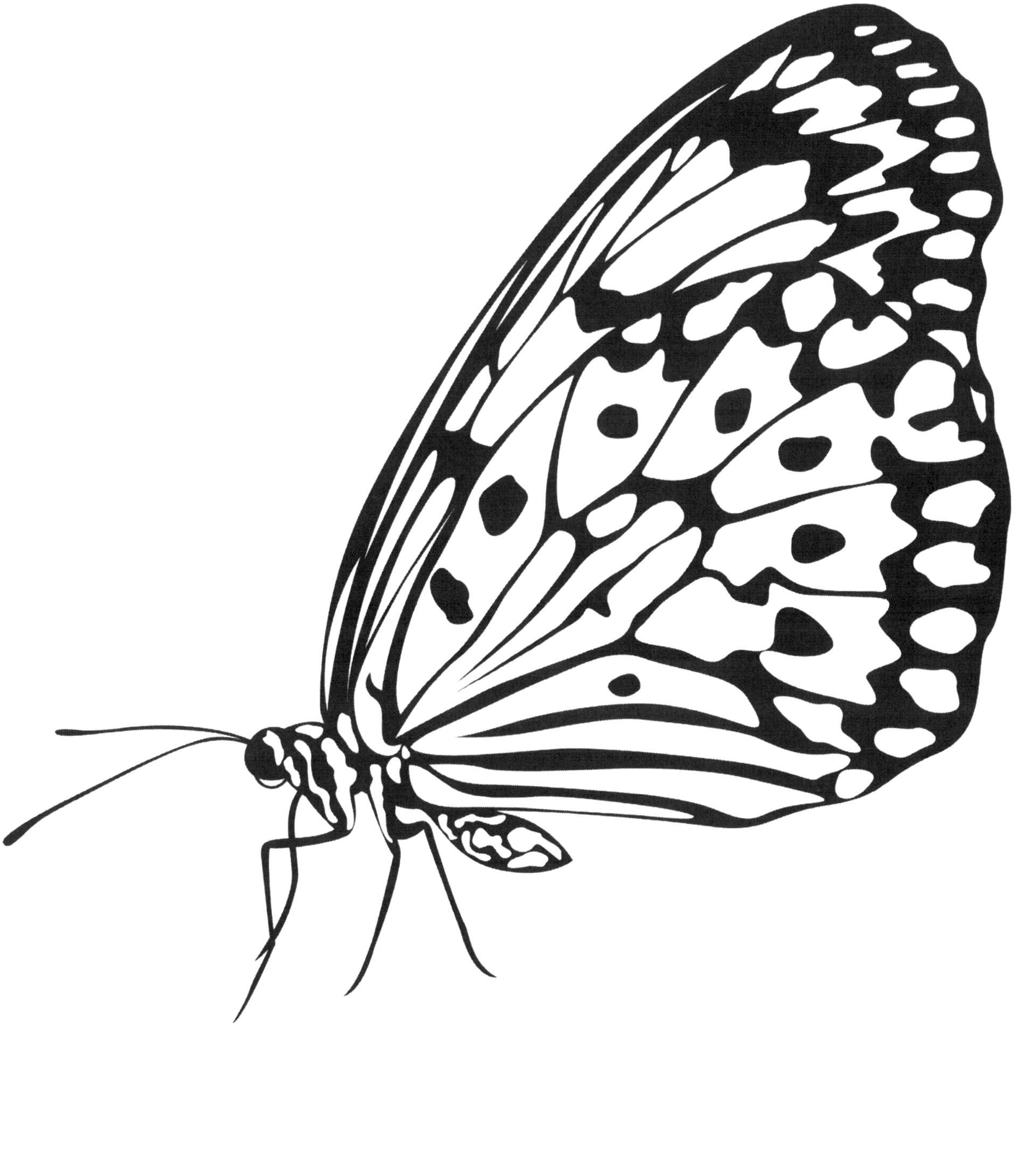

Date................................

Date ....

Date ....

Date ....

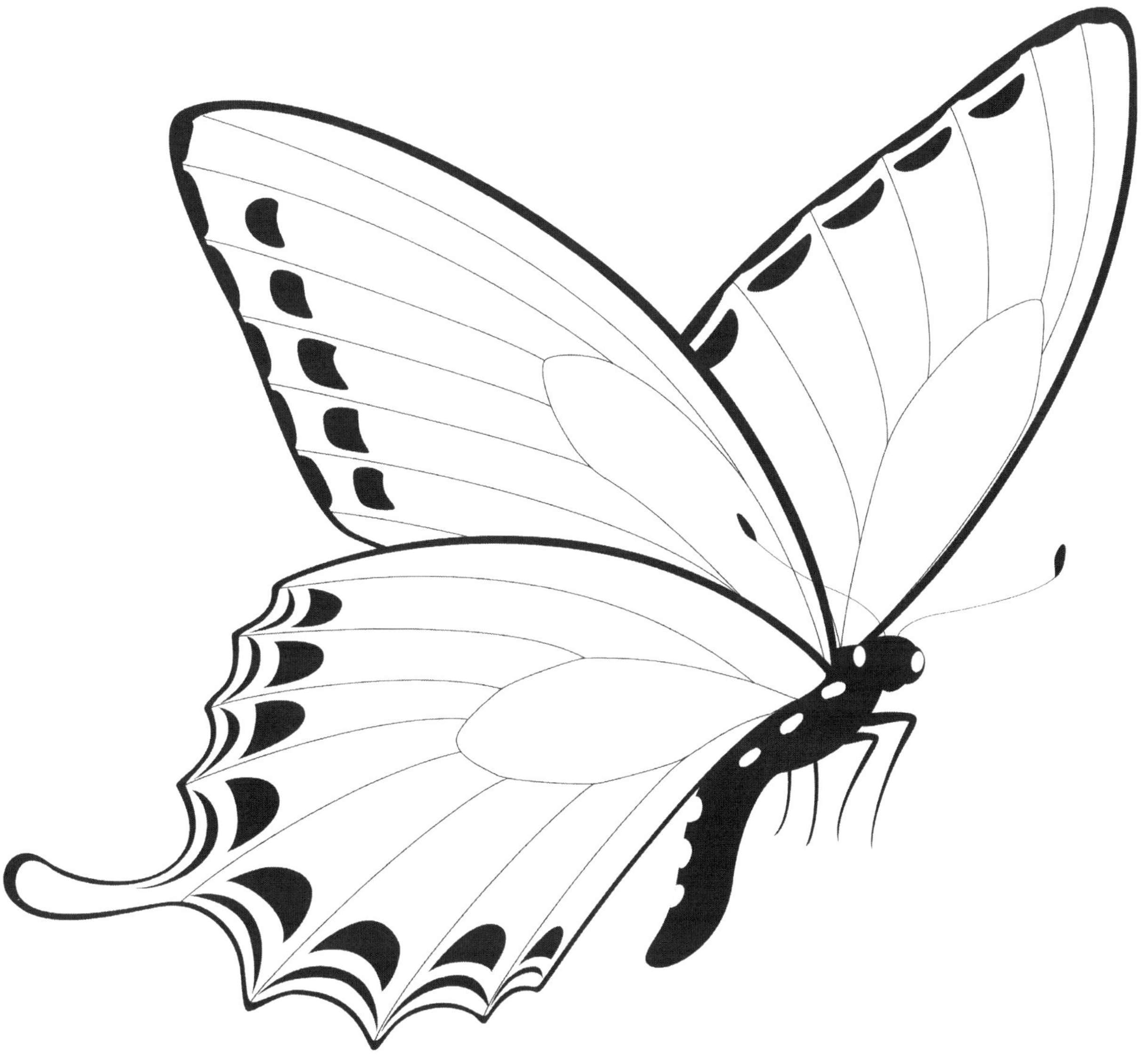

Date ....

Date ………………………………

Date ....

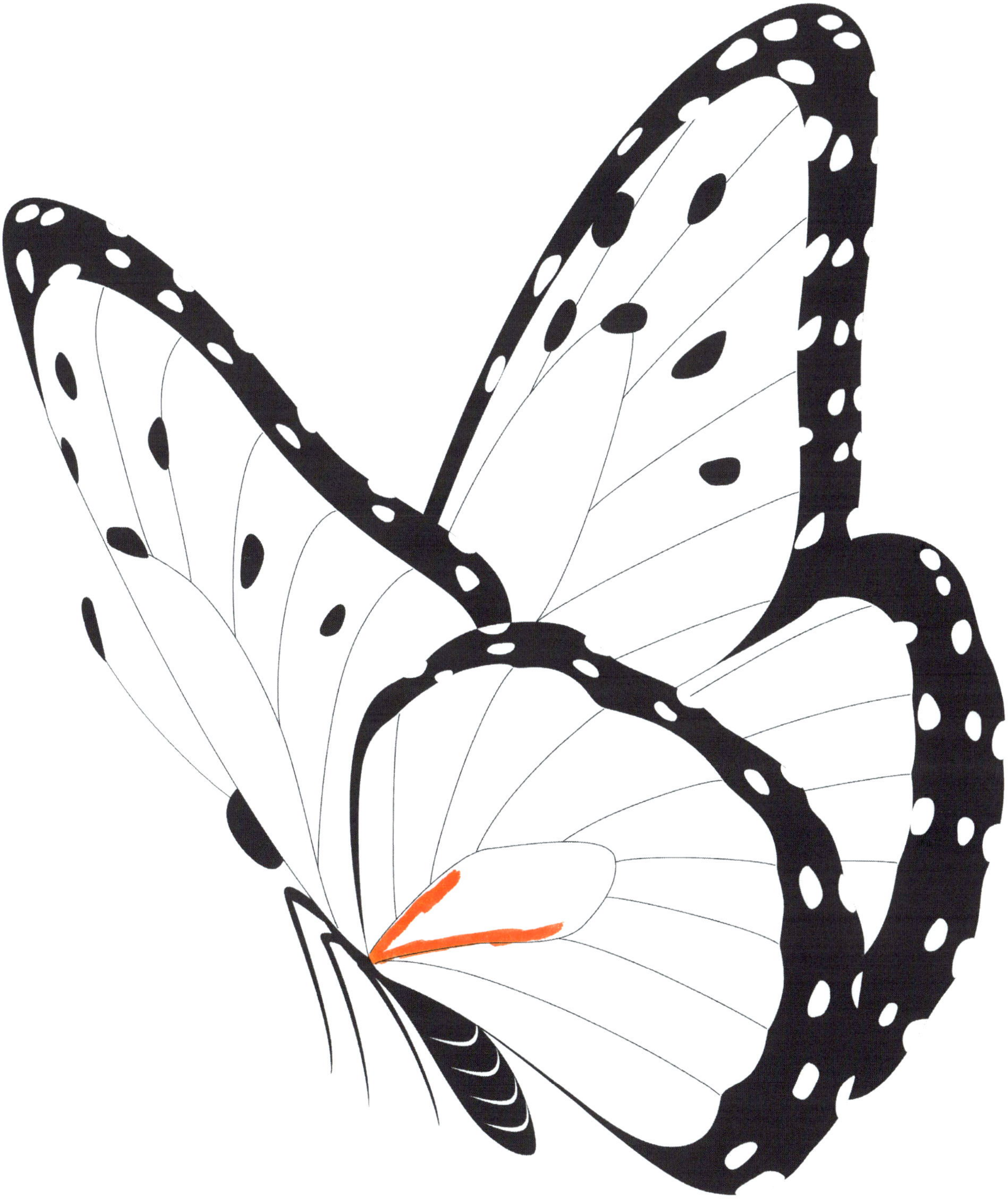

Date..................................

Date ....

Date ....

Date ....

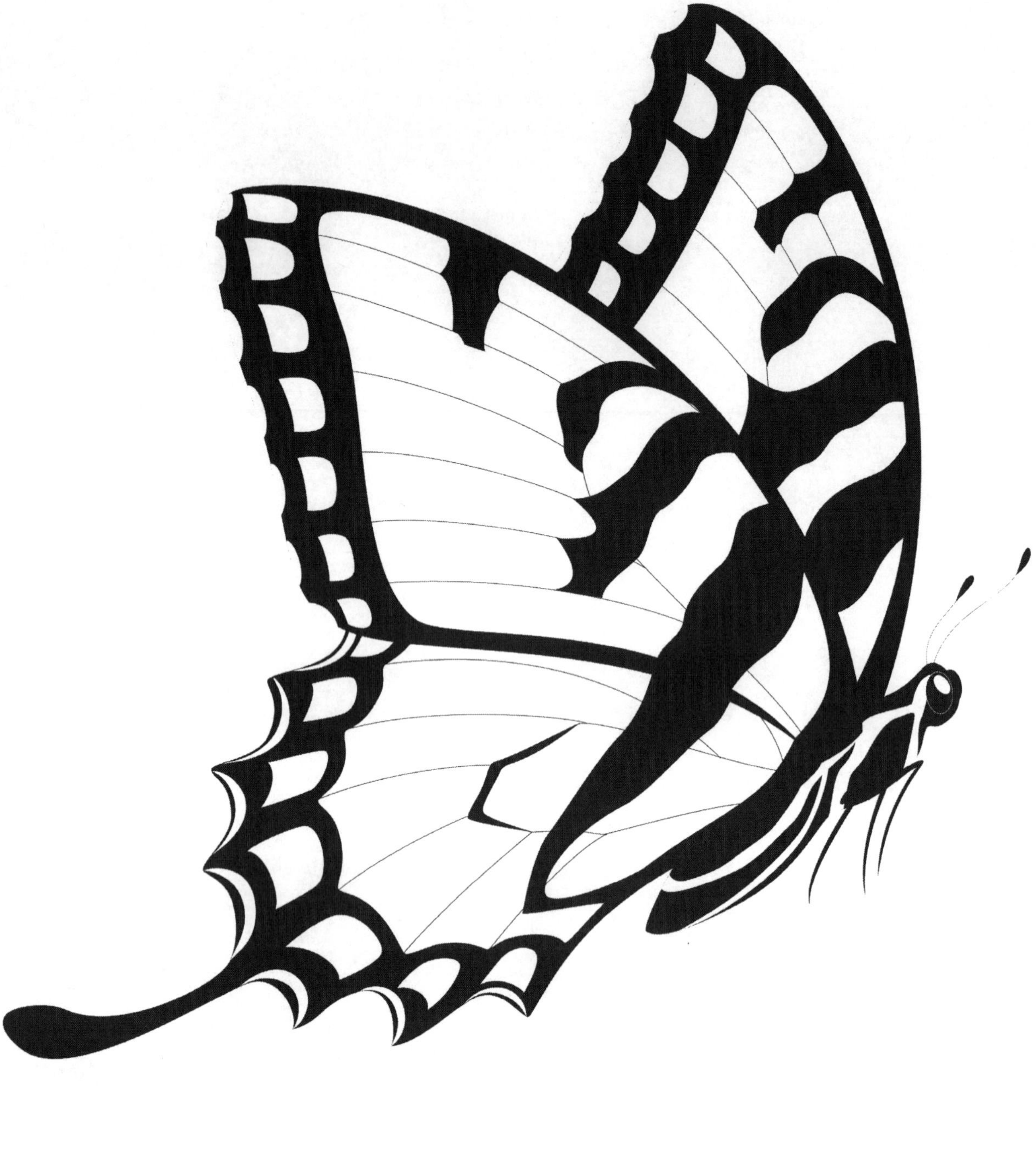

Date ....

Date ....

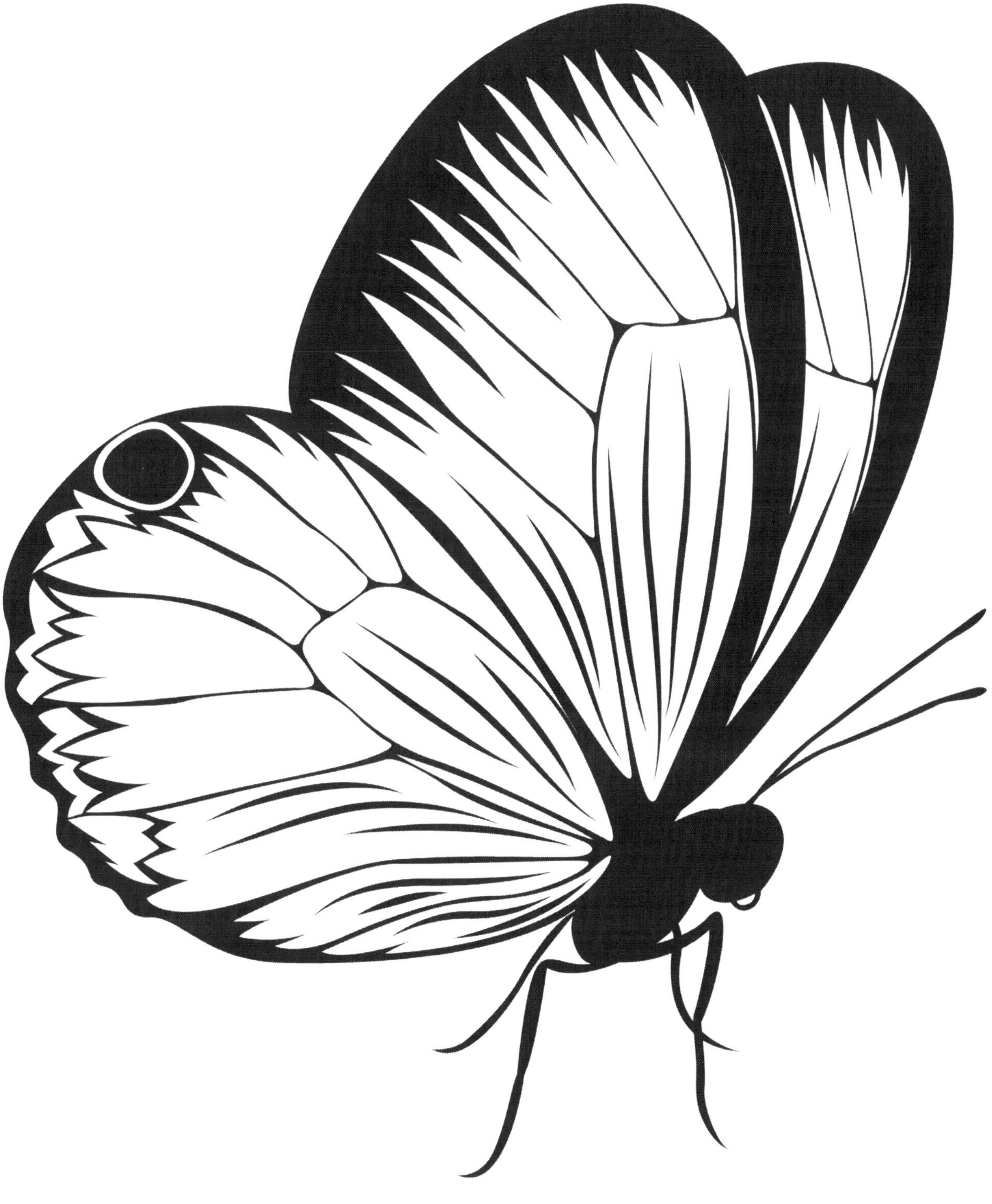

Date ....

Date ....

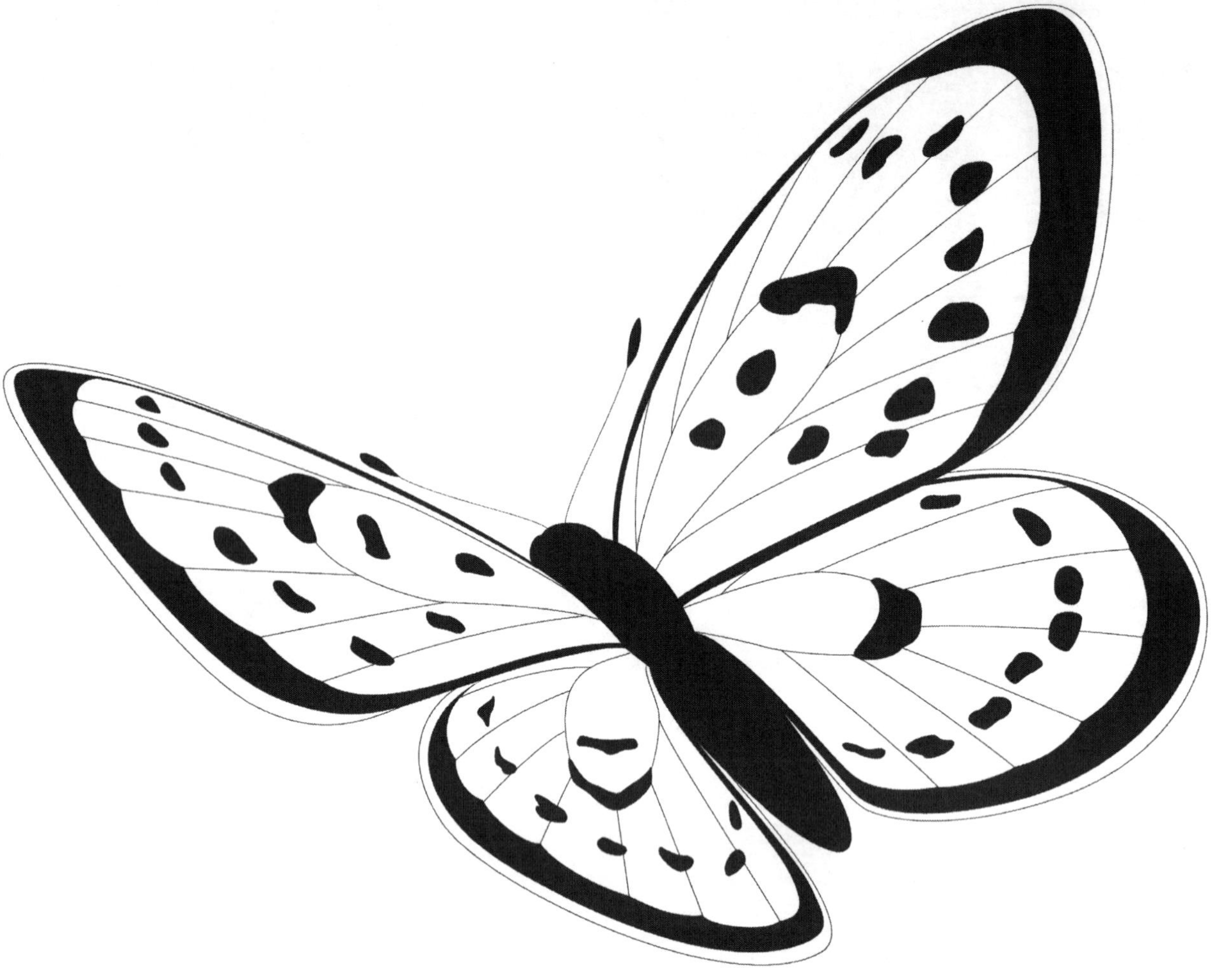

Date..................................

Date ....

Date ....

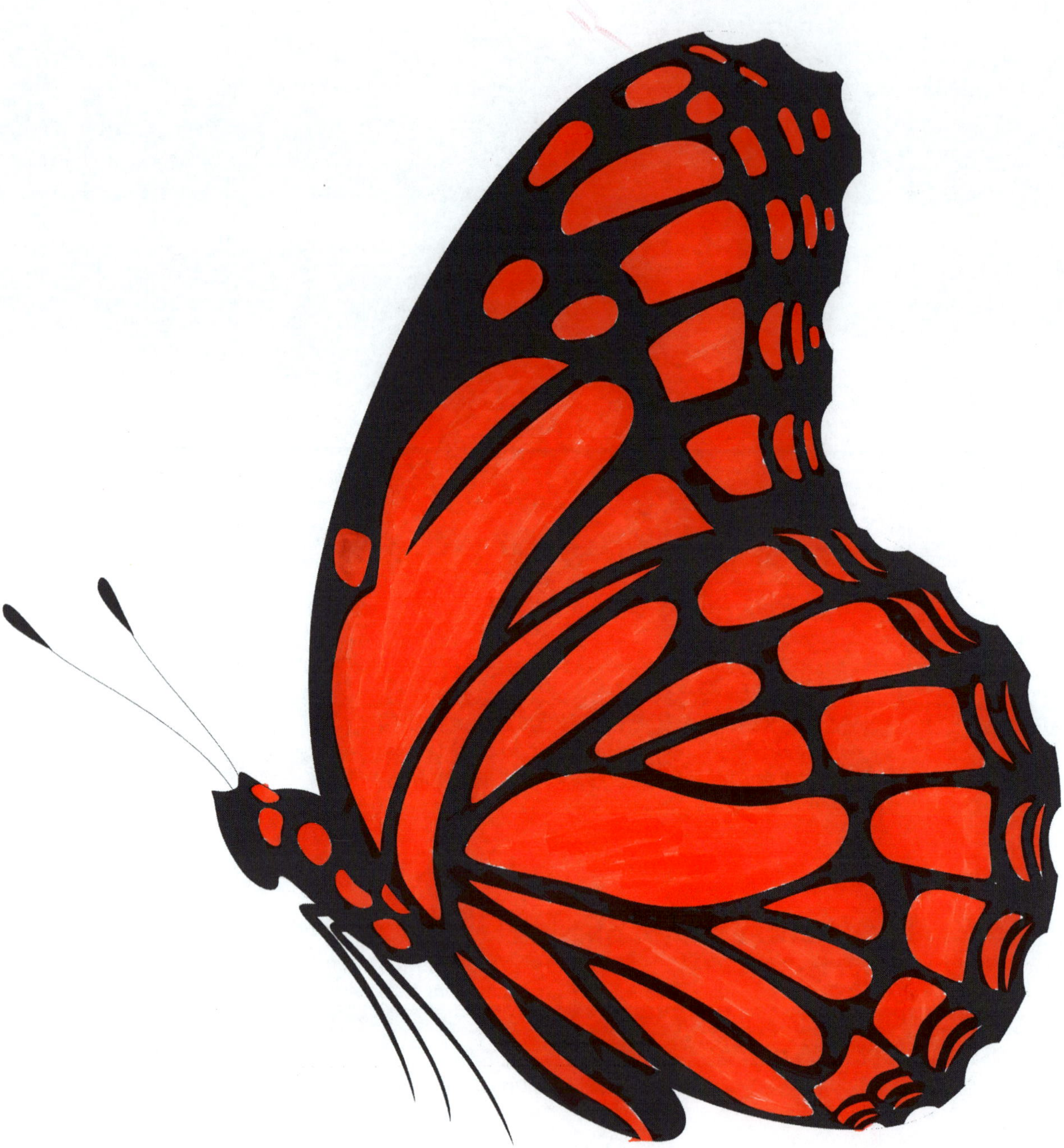

Date ....

Date ....

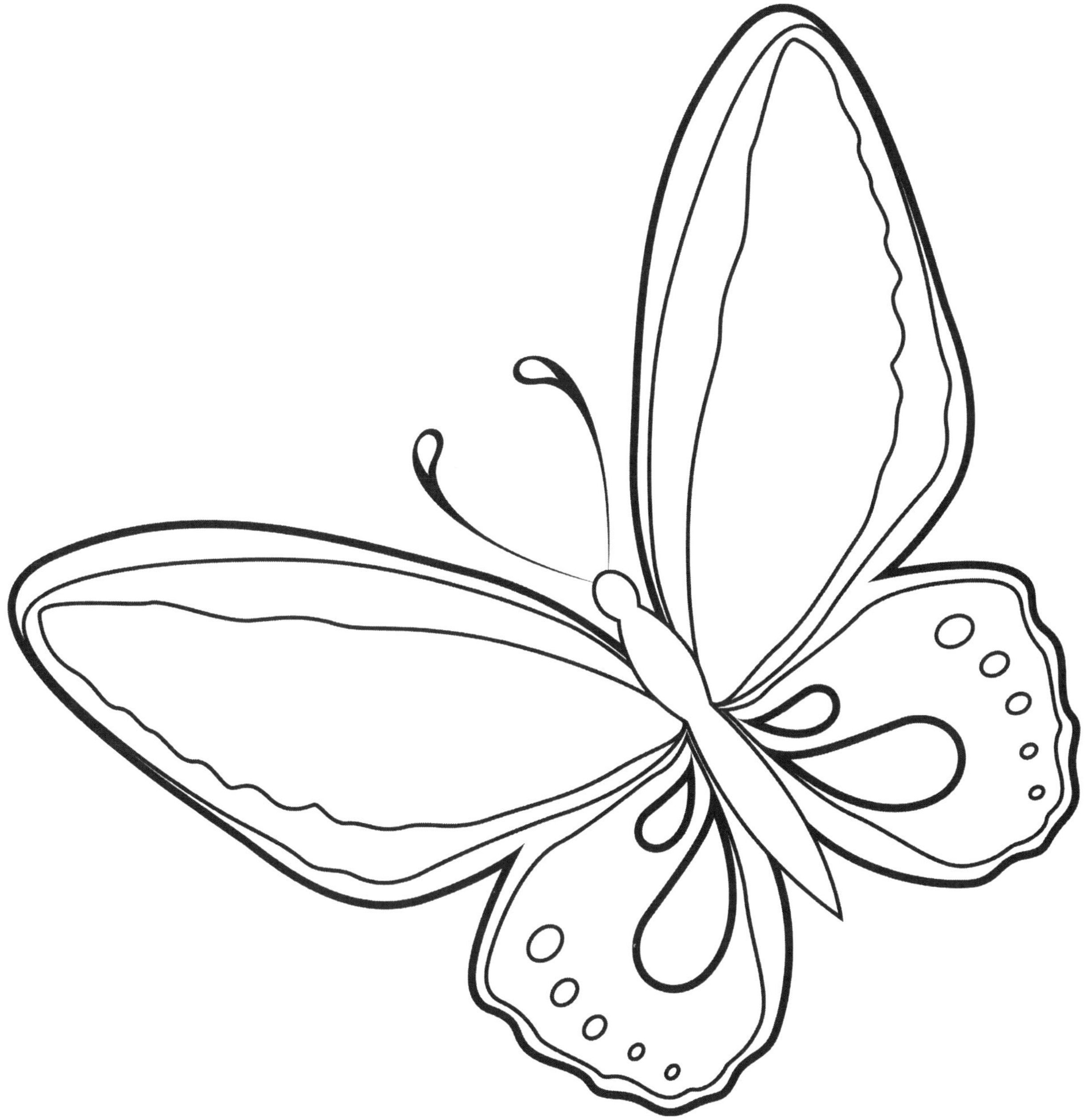

Date ....

Date ....

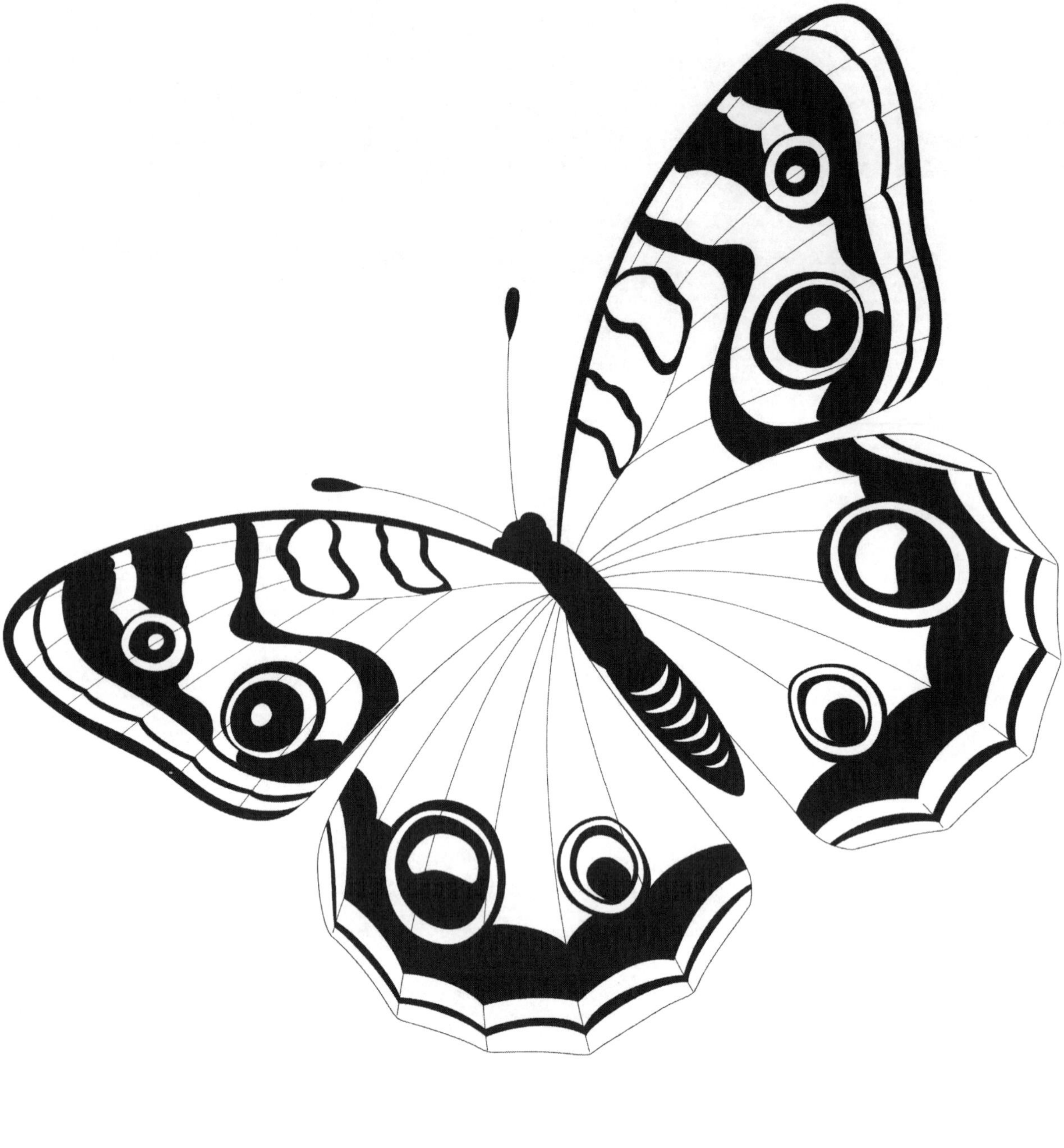

Date ....

Date ....

Date ....

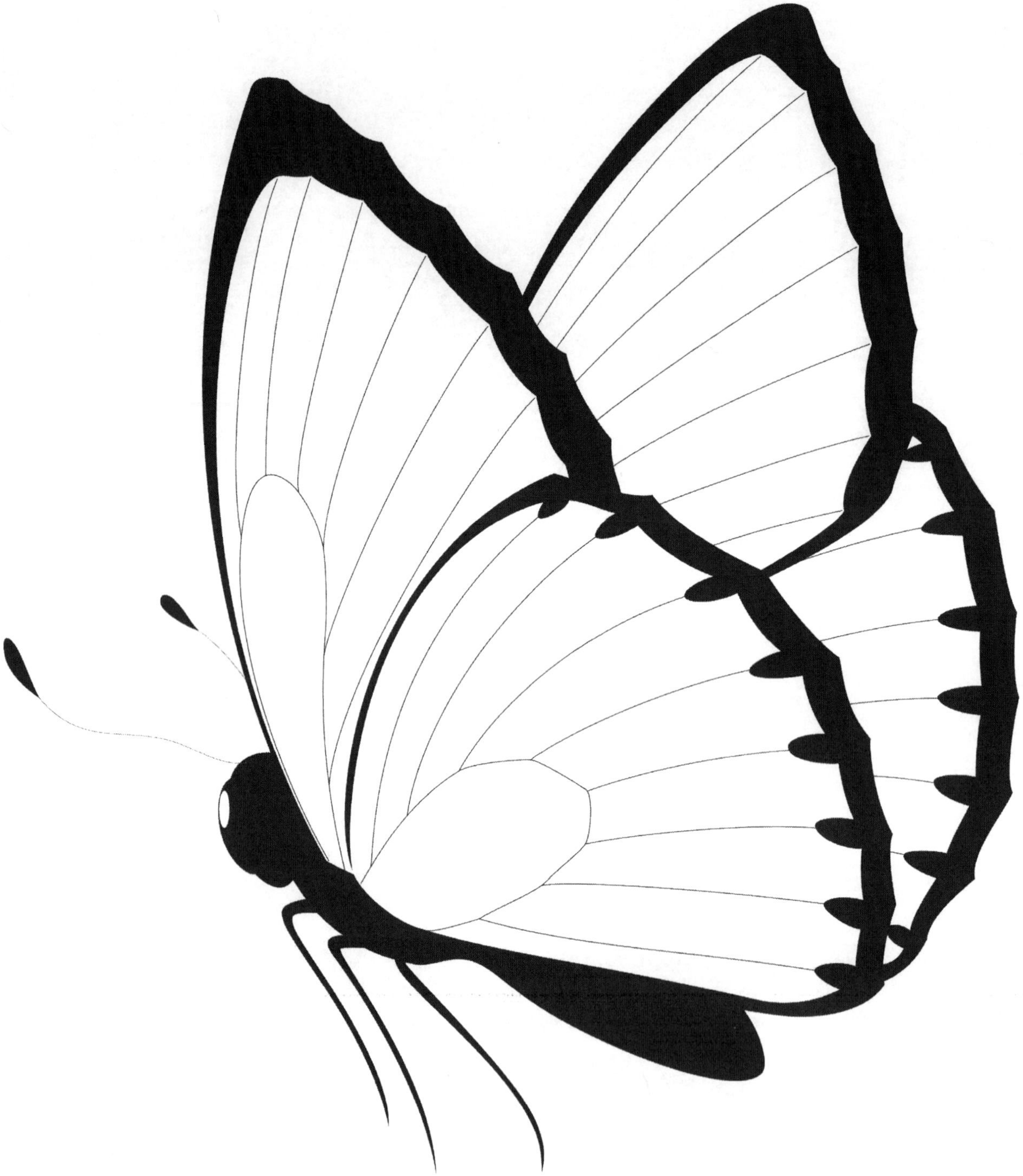

Date ....

Date ....

Date ....

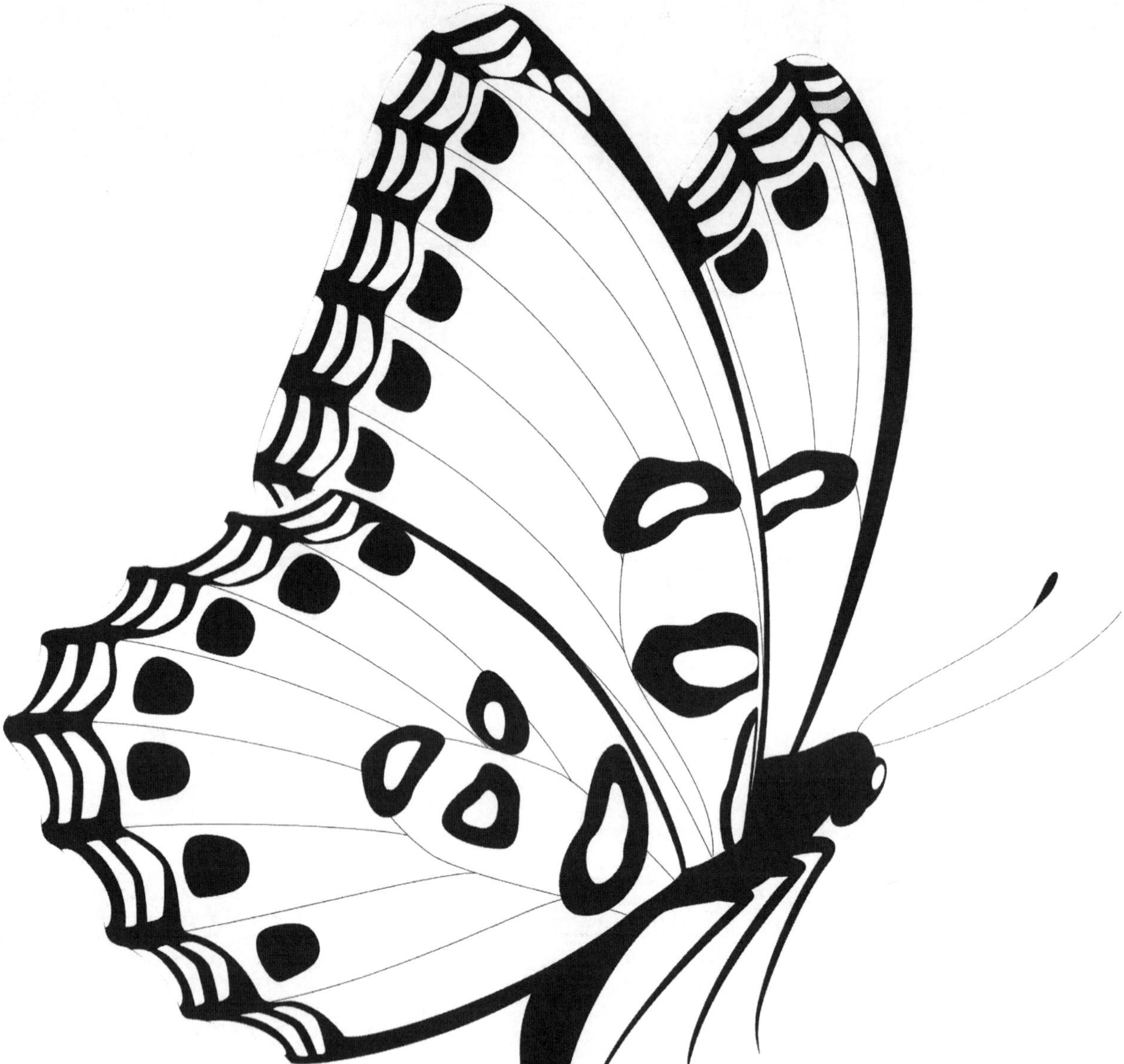

Date ....

Date ....

Date ....

Date ....

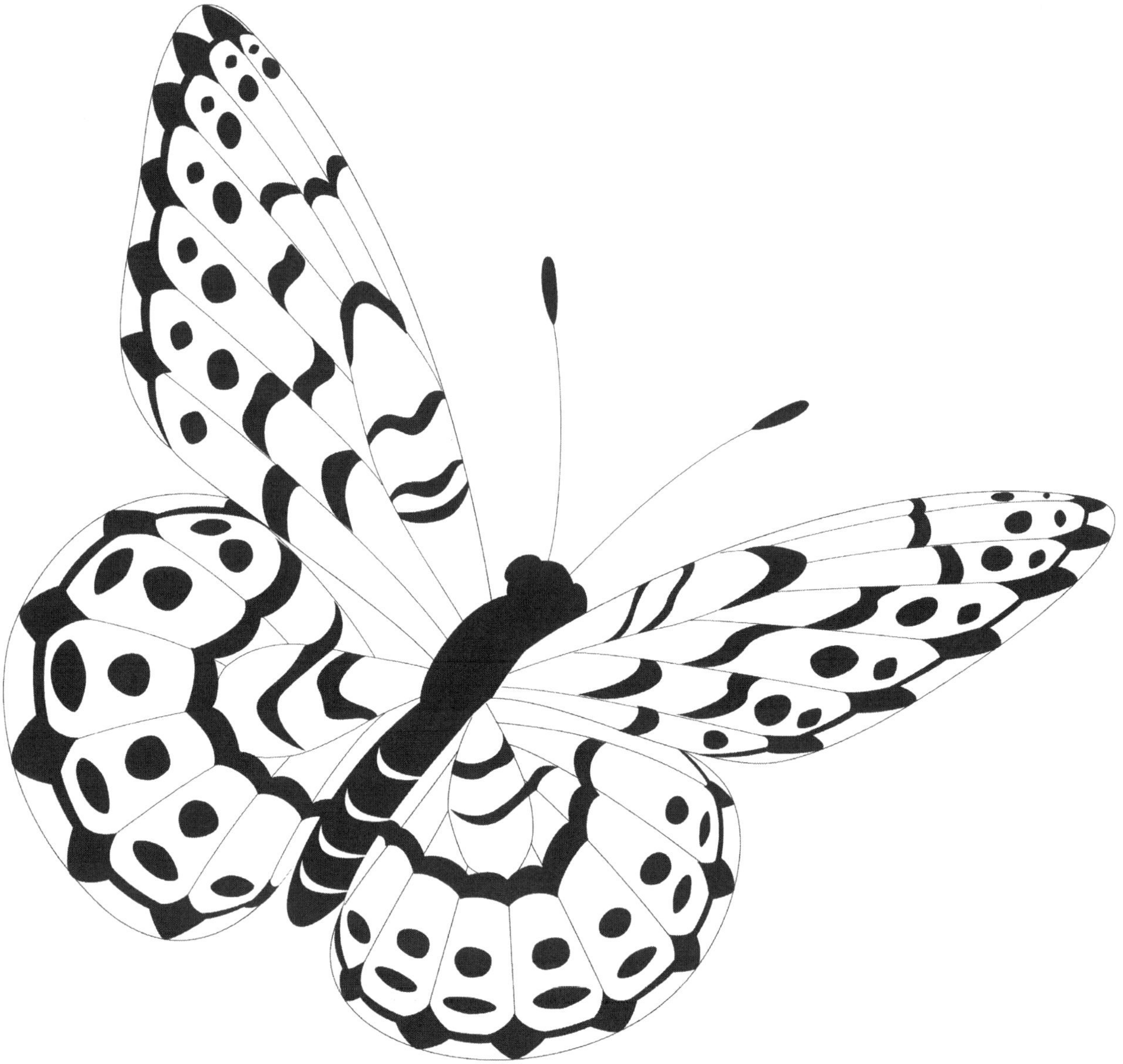

Date ....

Date ....

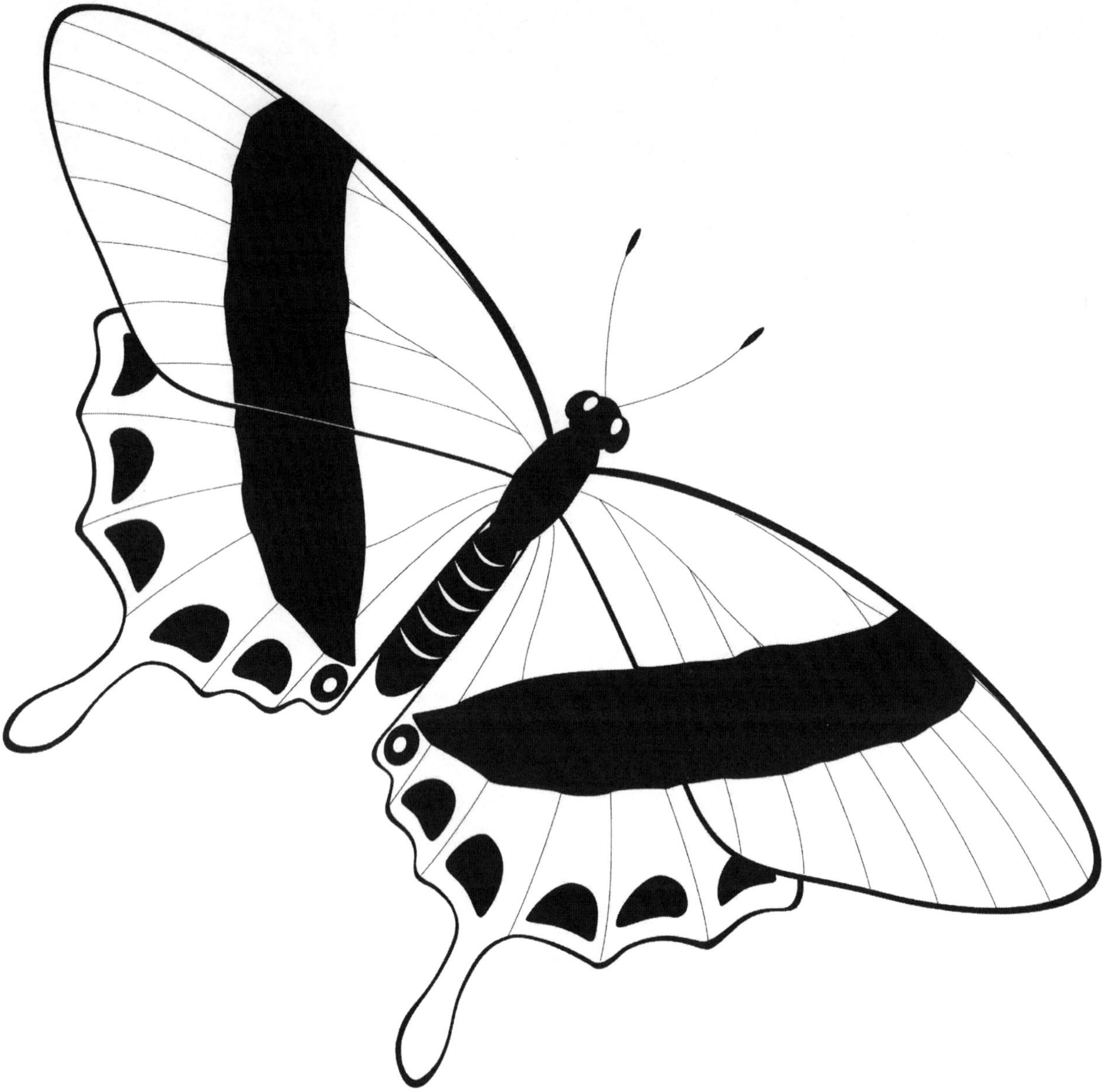

Date ....

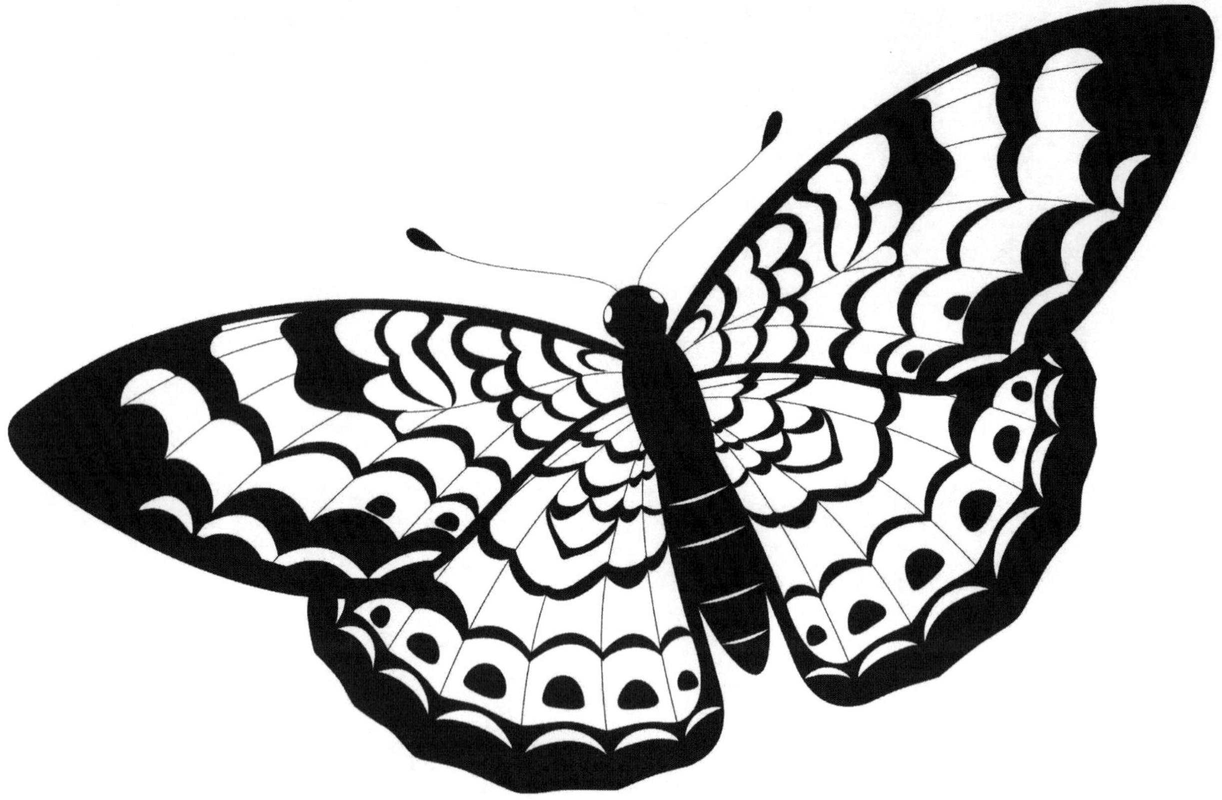

Date ....

Date ....

Date ....

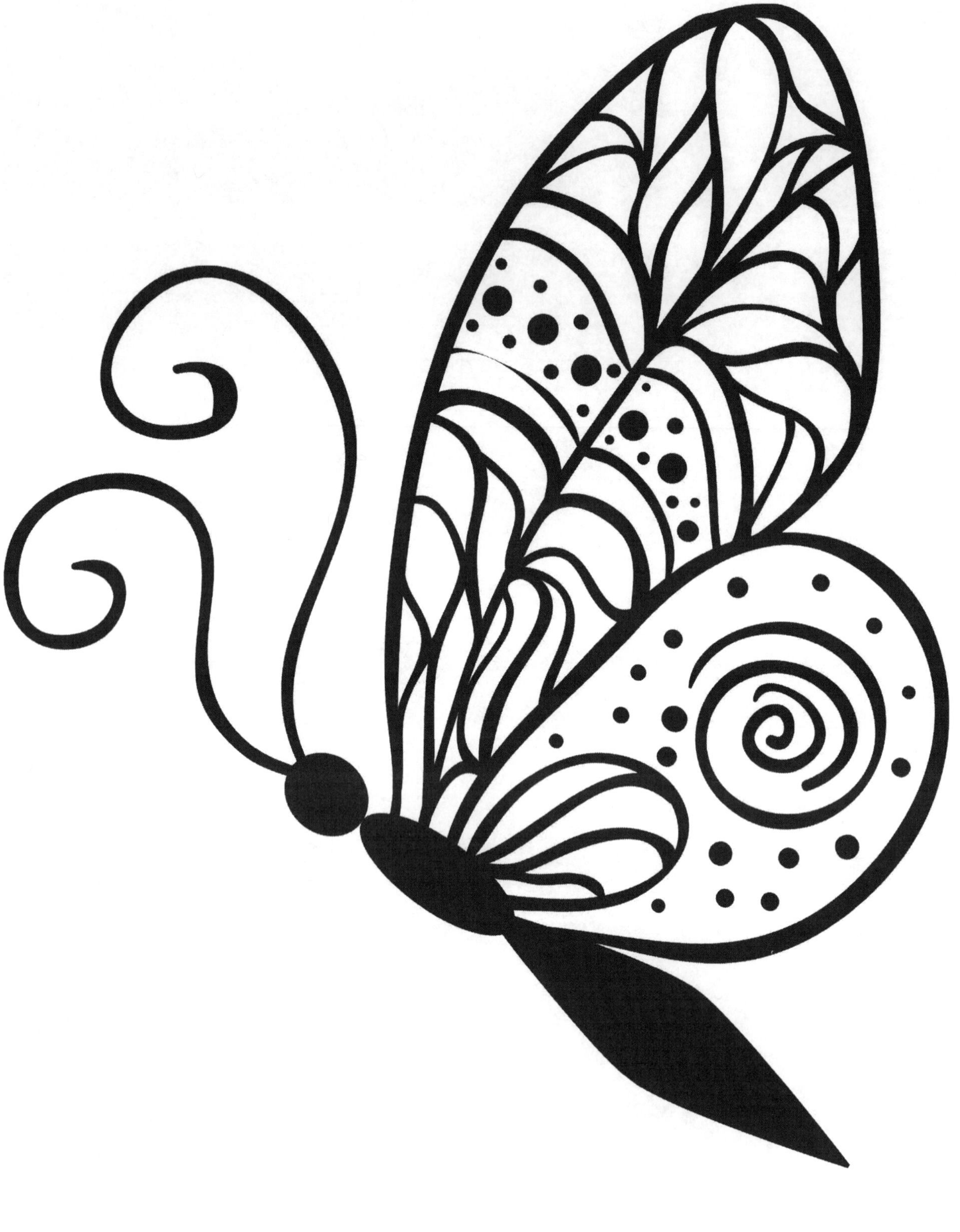

Date ……………………………………

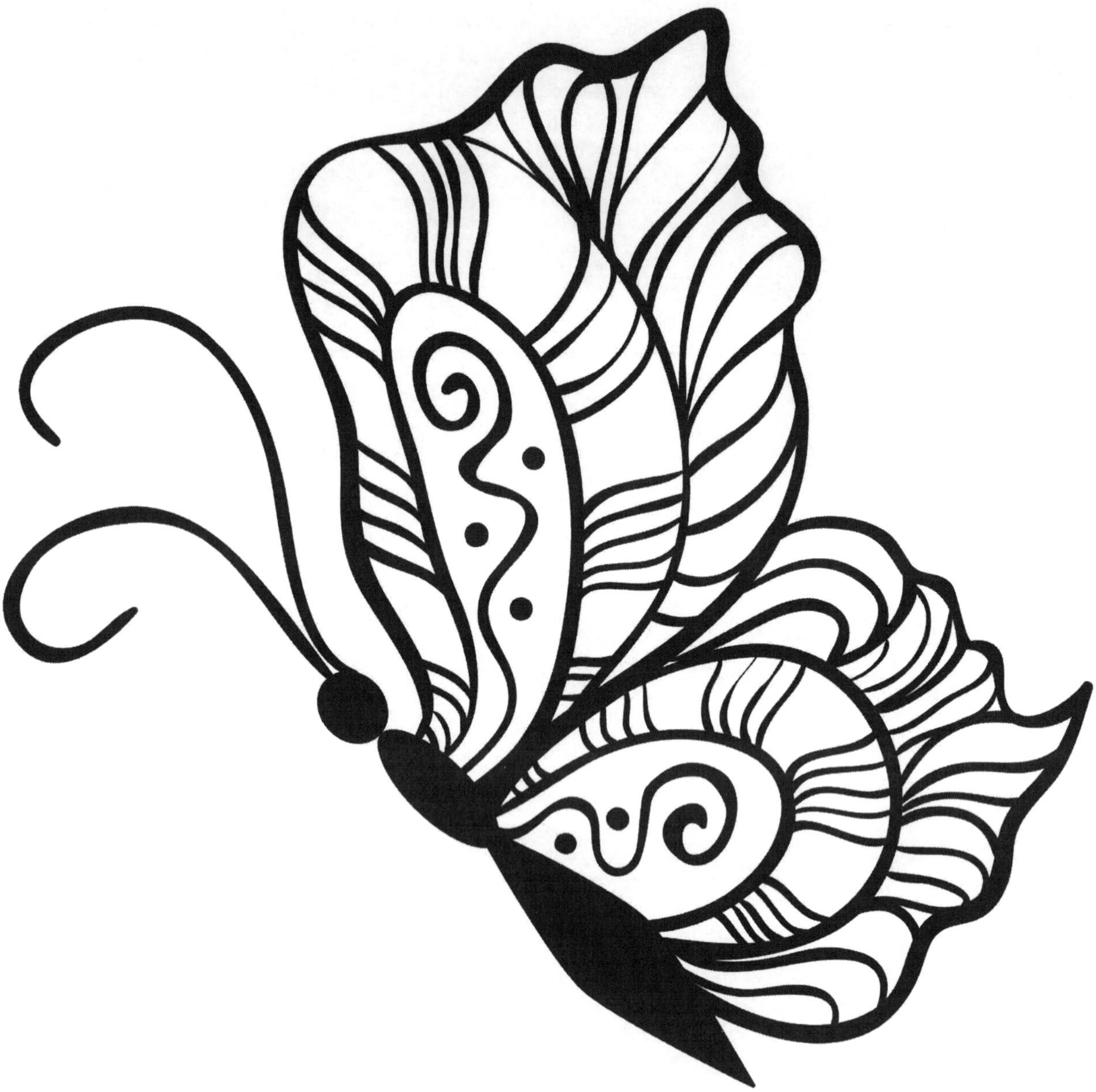

Date ....

Date ……………………………….

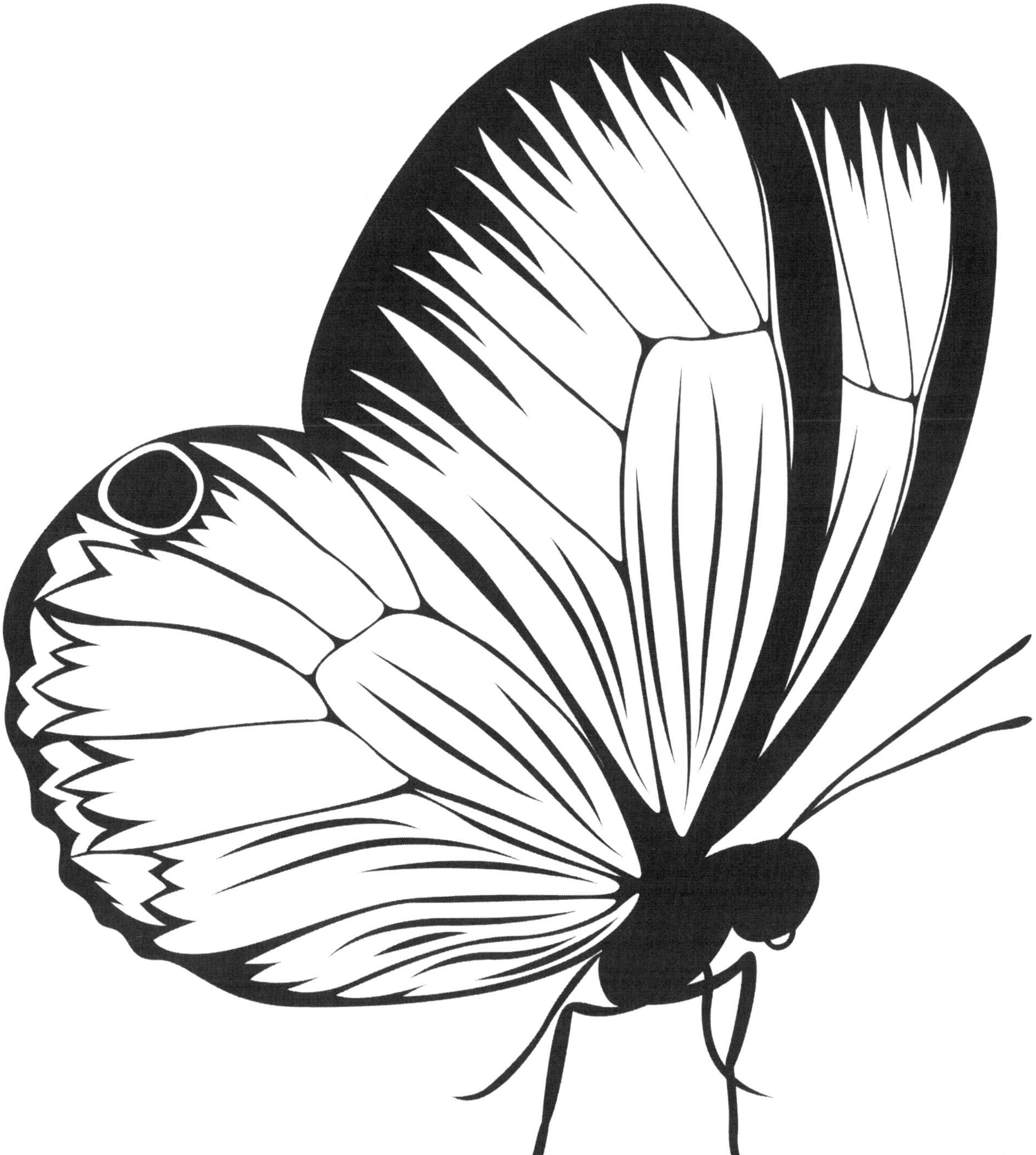

Date ....

Date ....

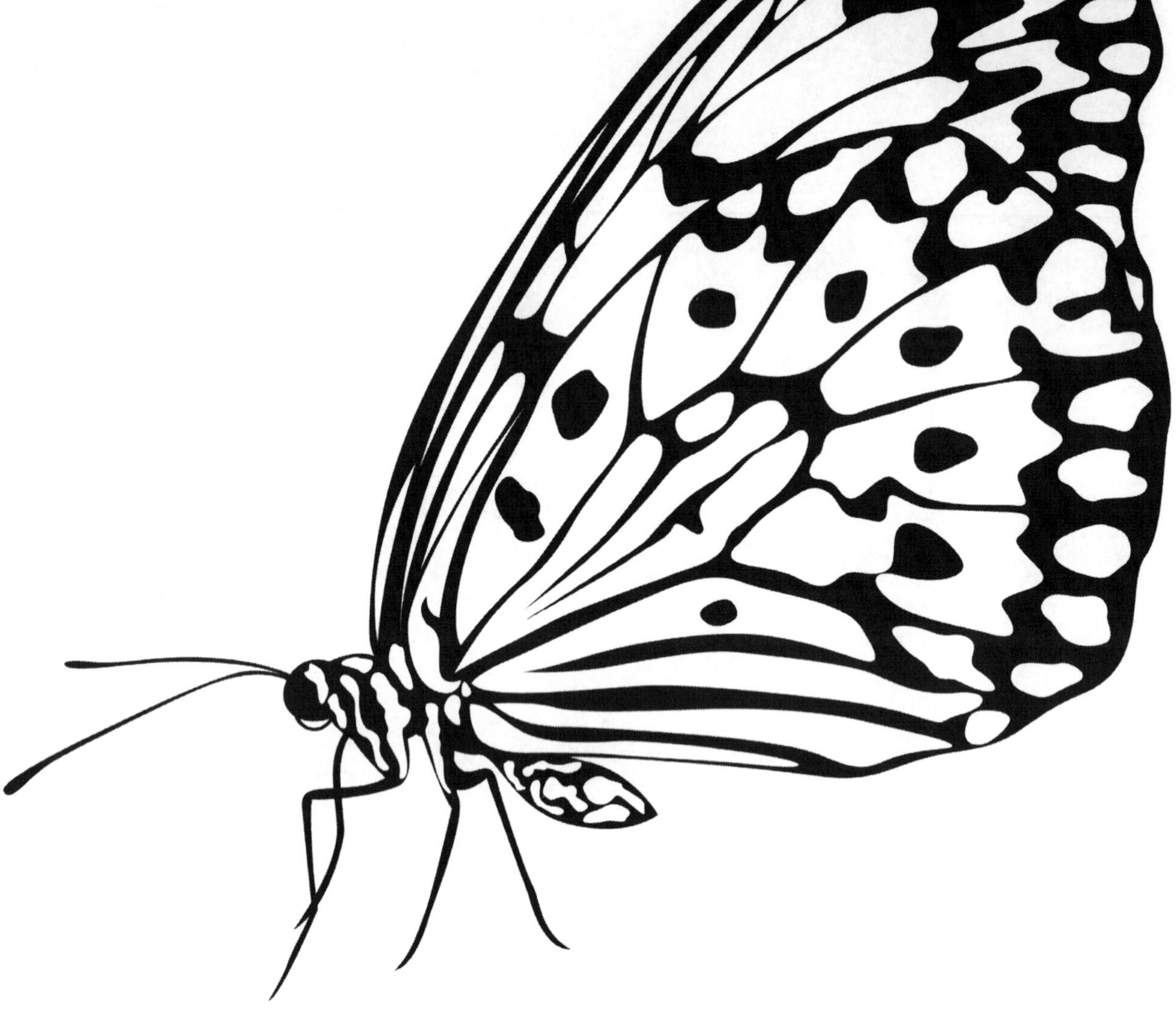

Date ....

Date ....

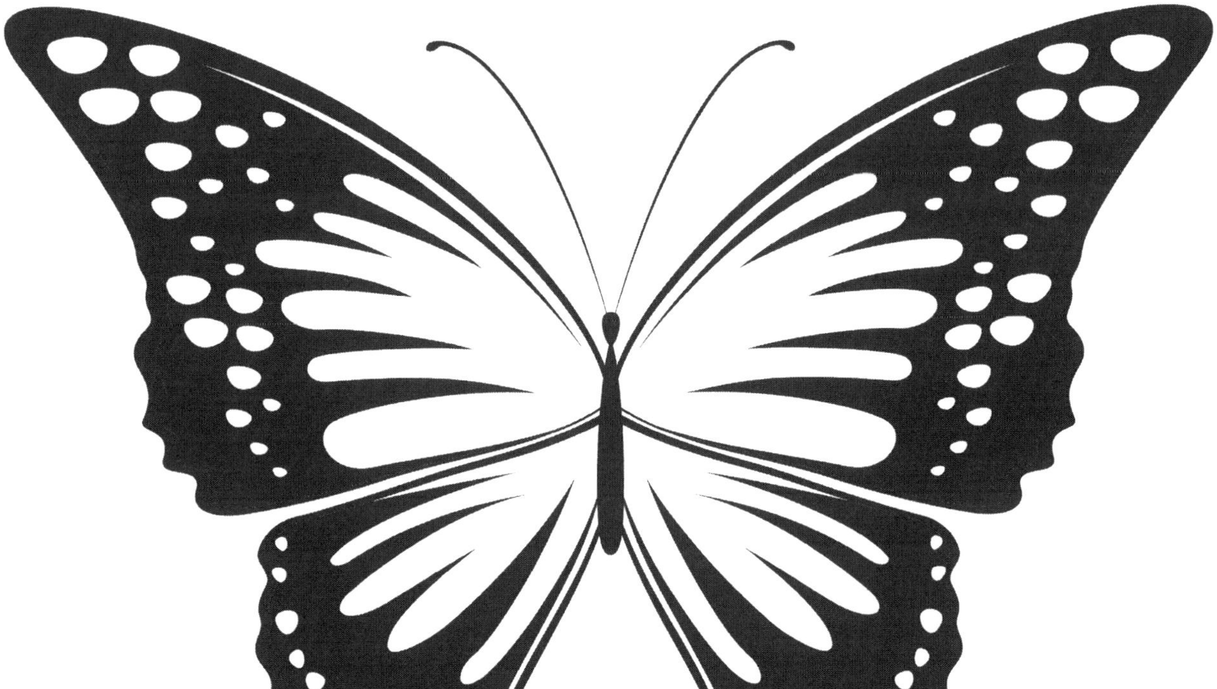

Date ....

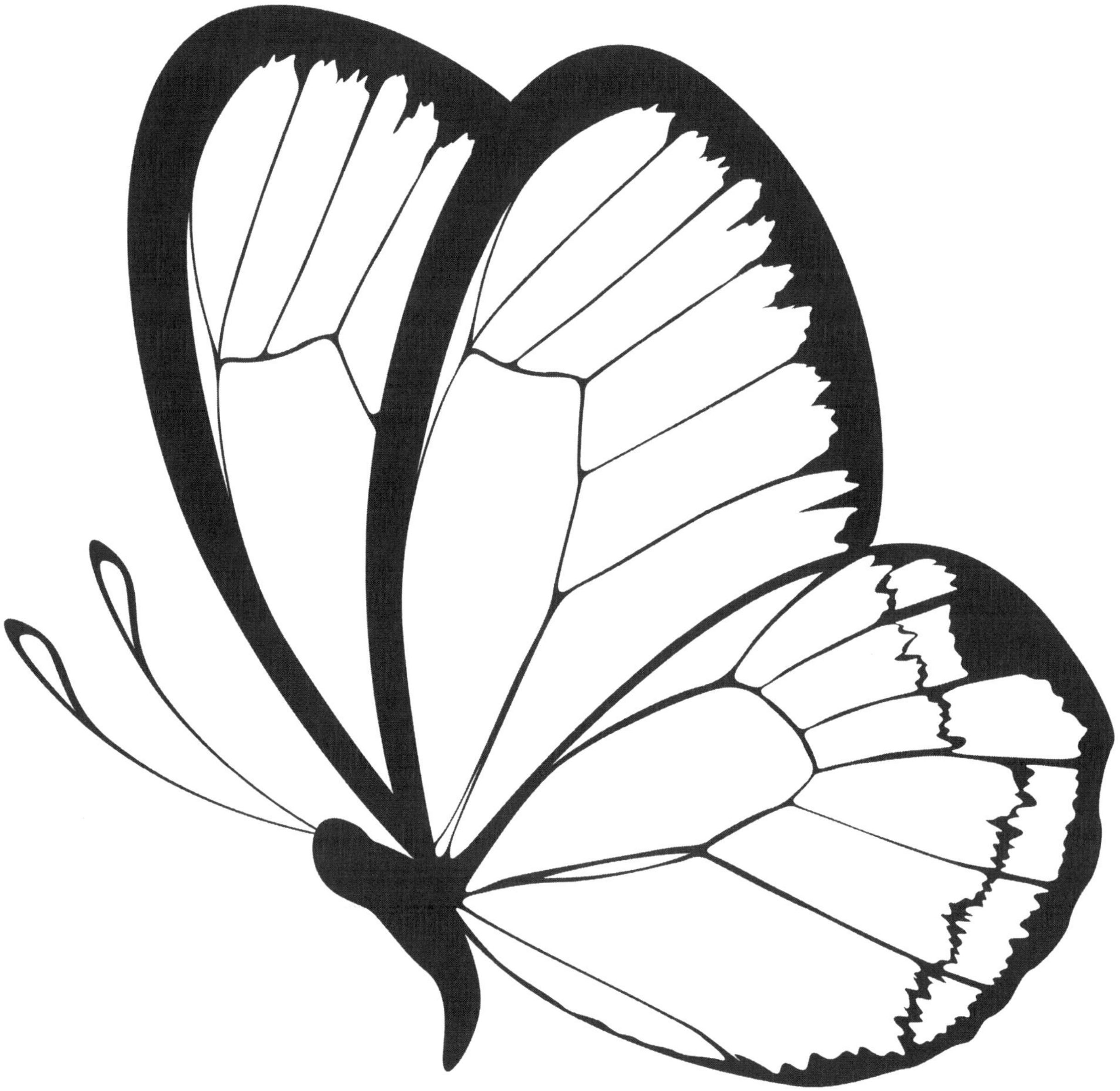

Date ....

Date ....

Date……………………………

Date ....

Date ....

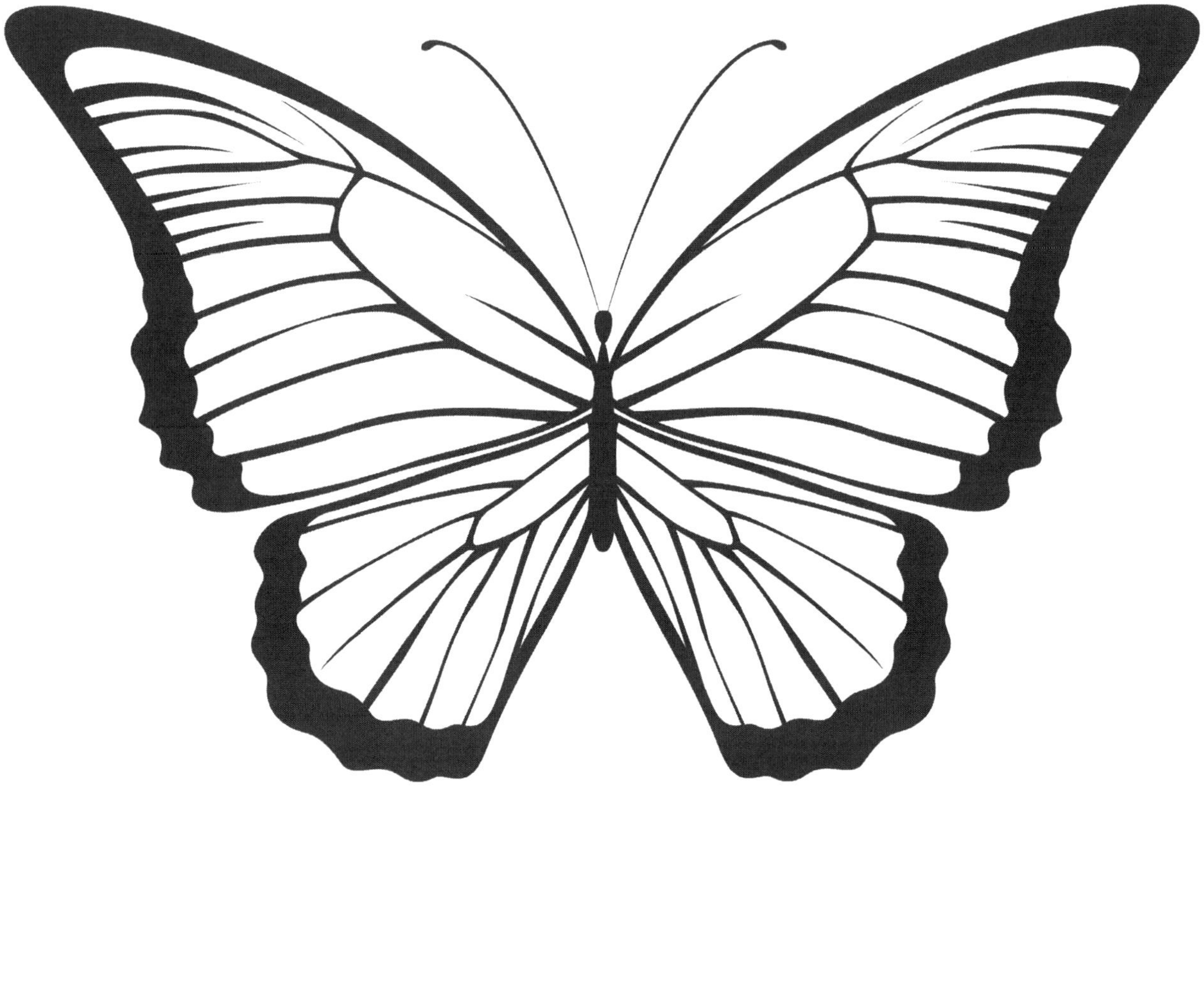

Date ....

Date ....

Date ....

Date..............................

Date ....

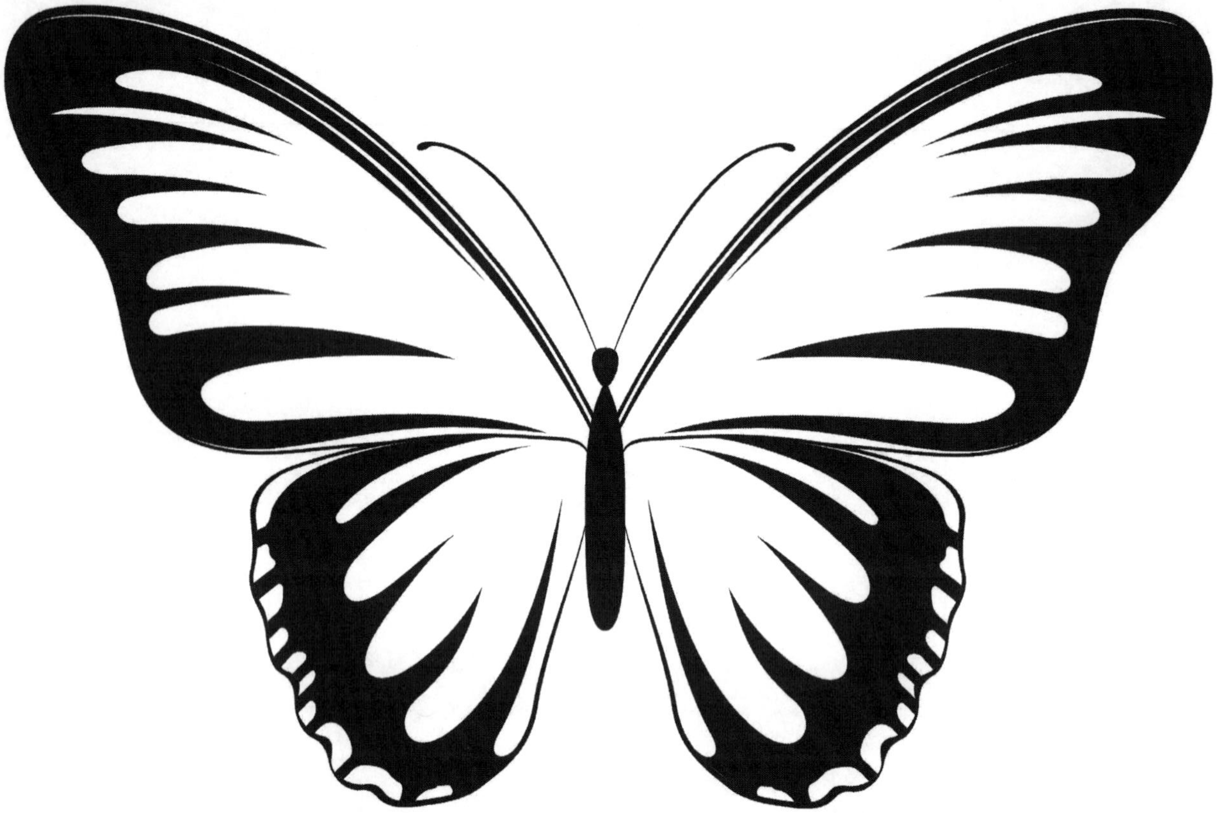

Date ....

Date ....

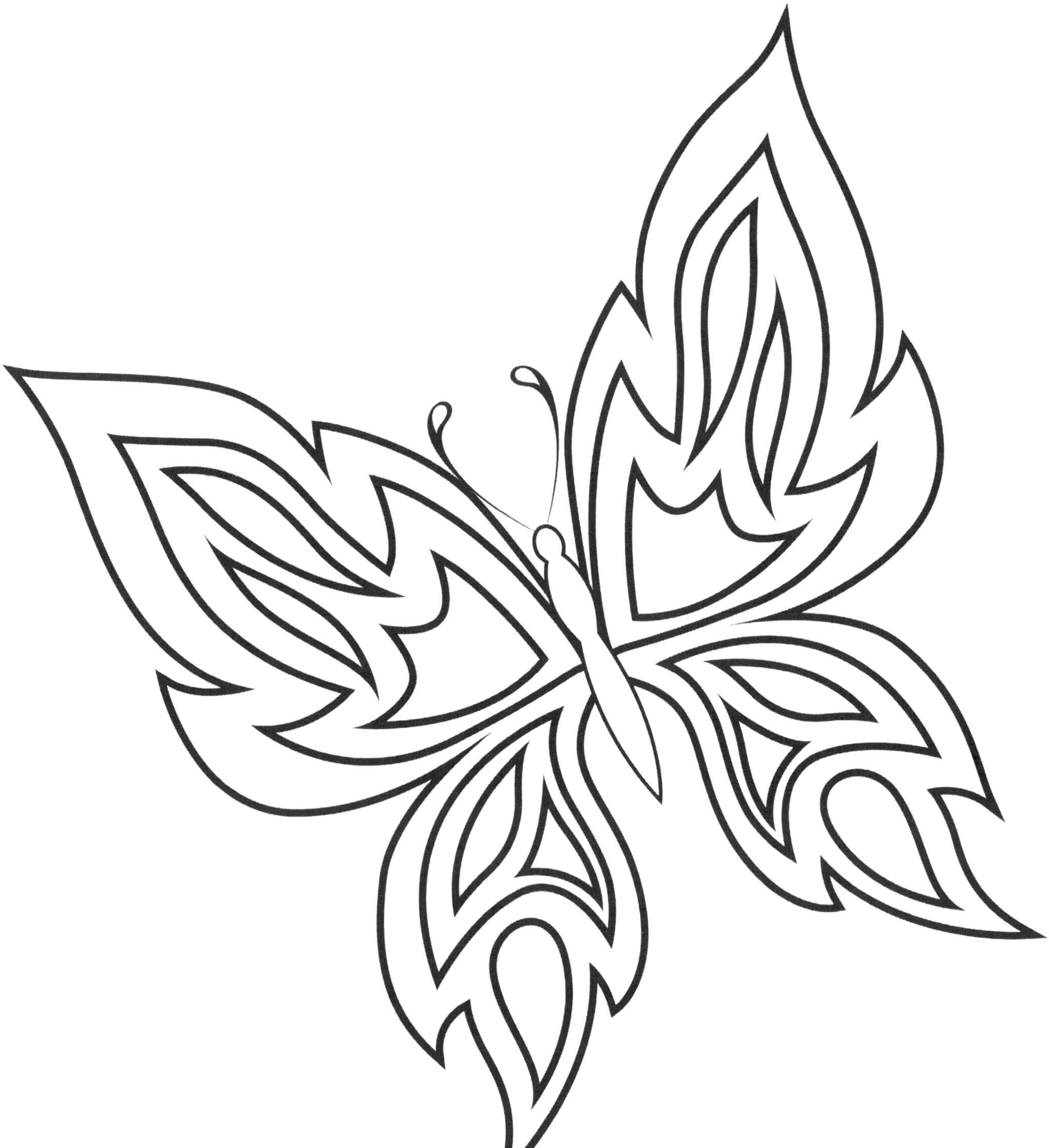

Date ....

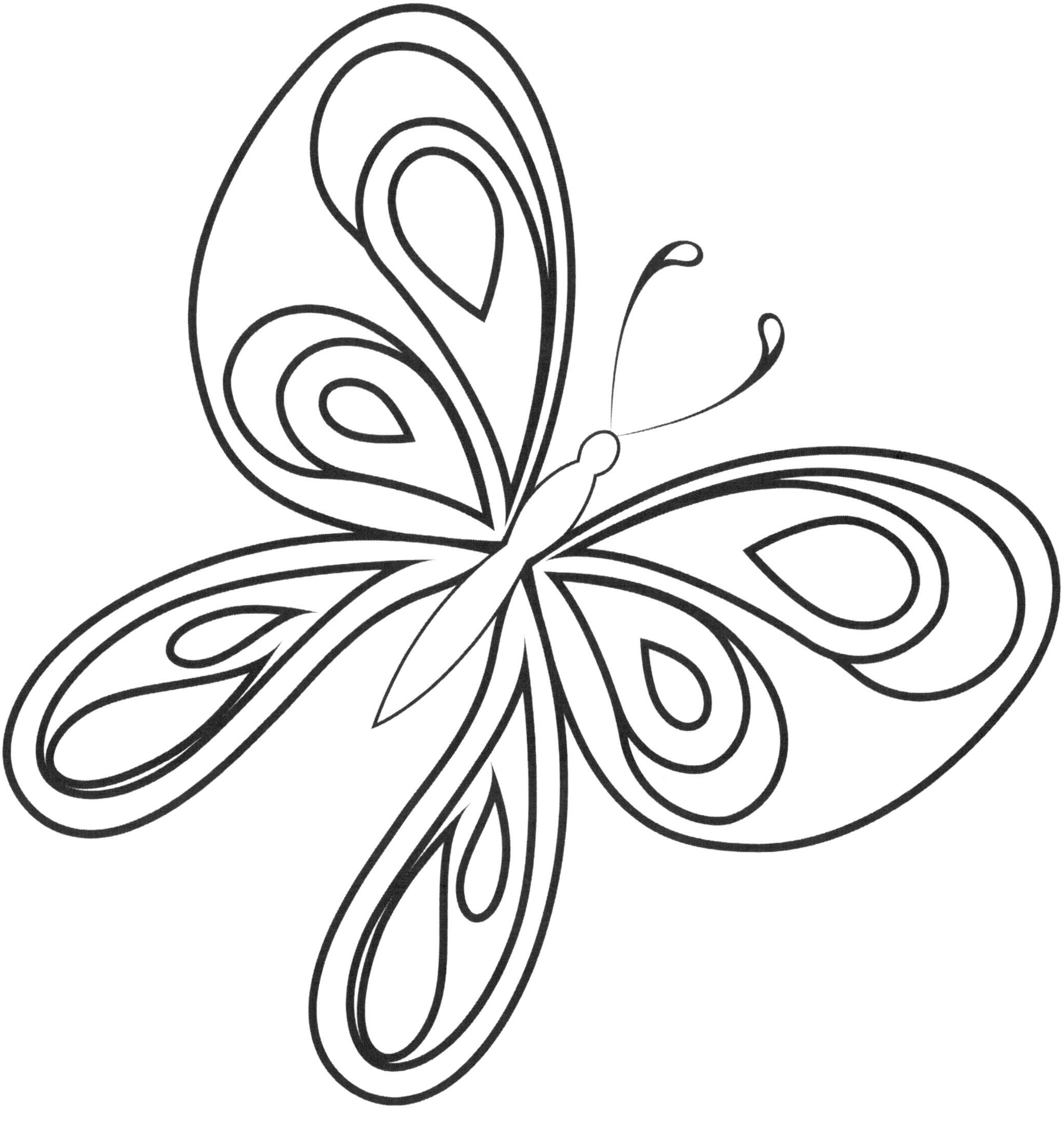

Date ....

Date ....

Date ....

Date ....

Date…………………………………

Date……………………………………

Date ....

Date..................................

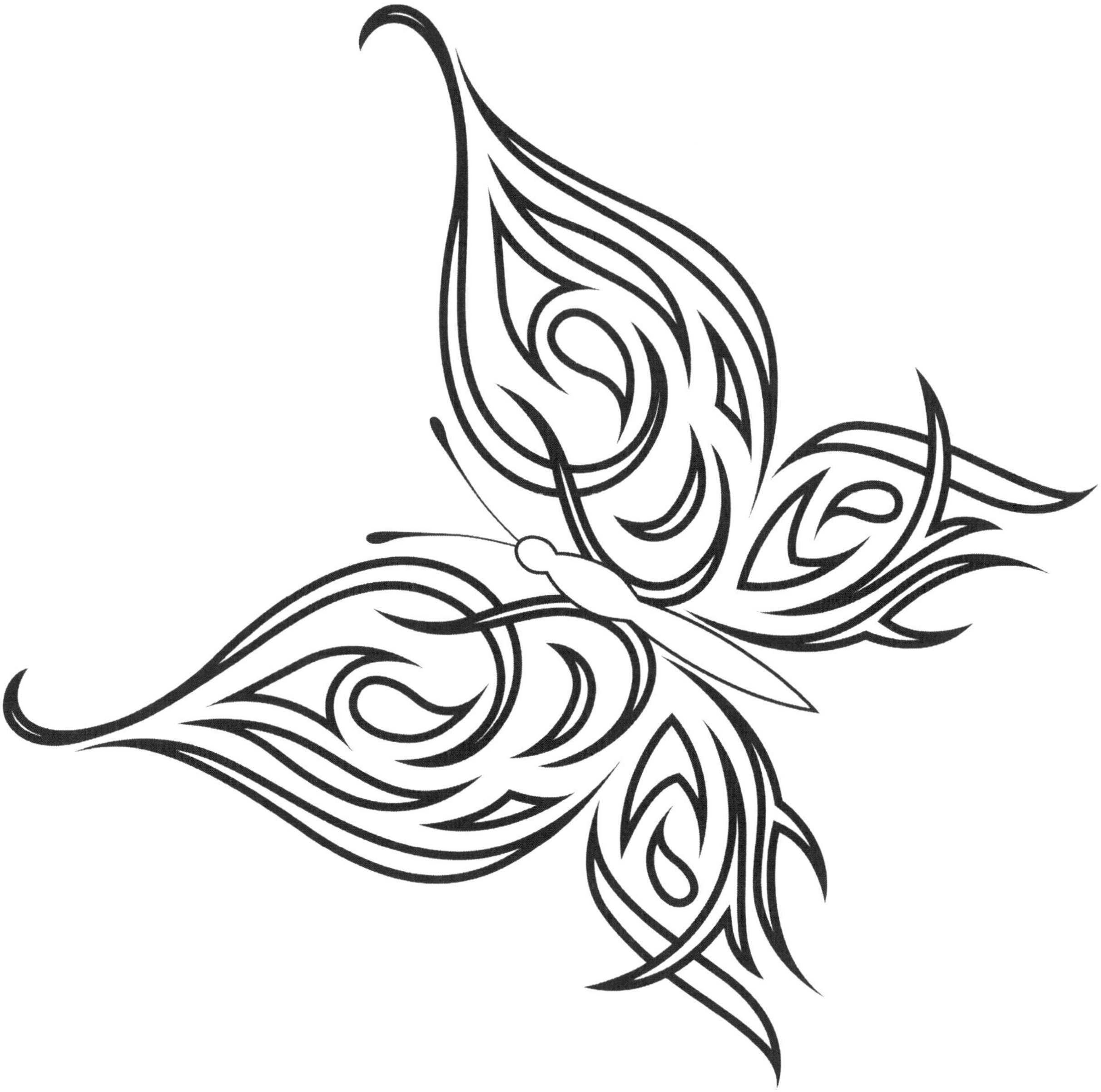

Date ....

Date ....

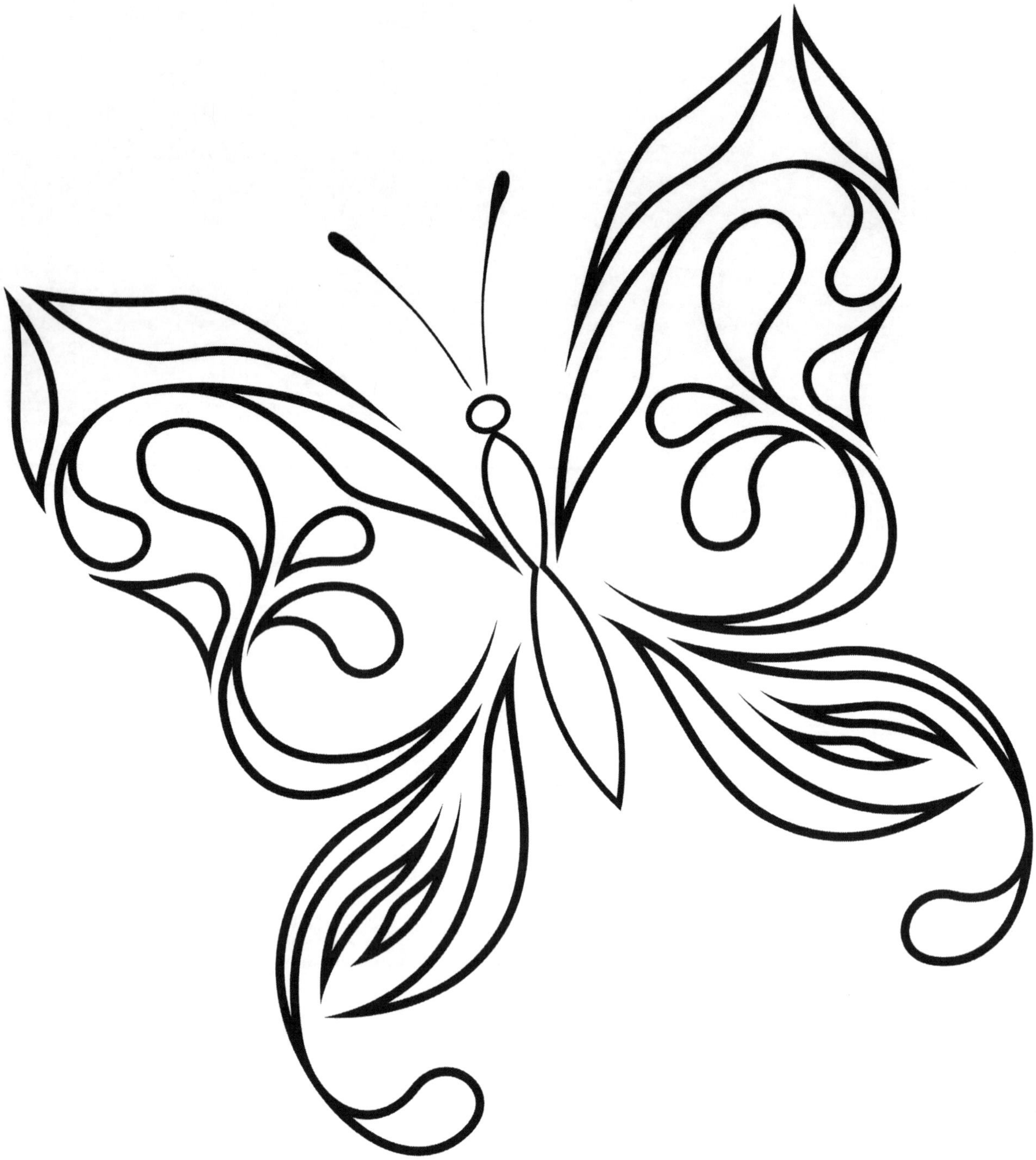

Date ....

Date ....

Date ....

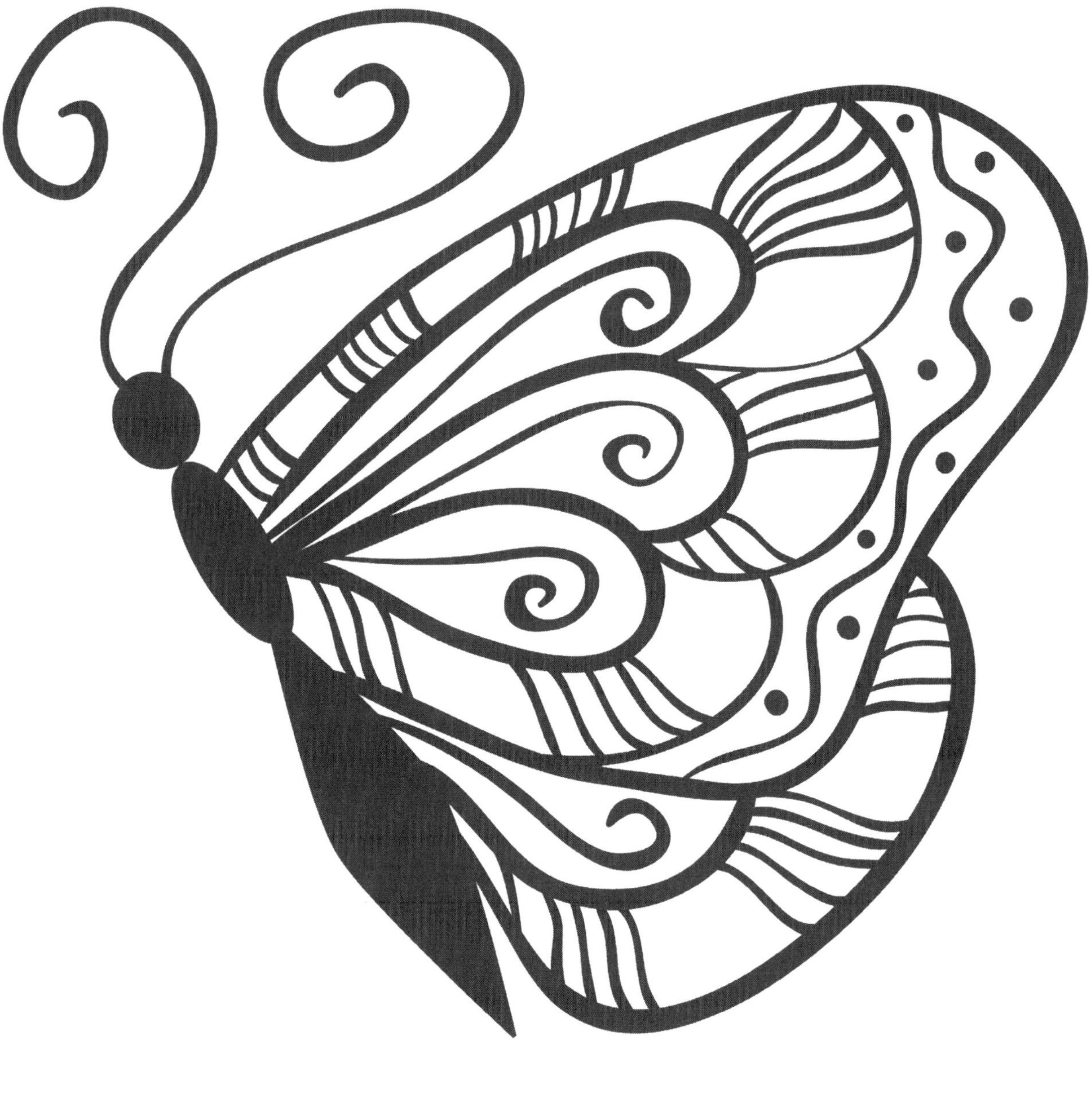

Date ....

Date ....

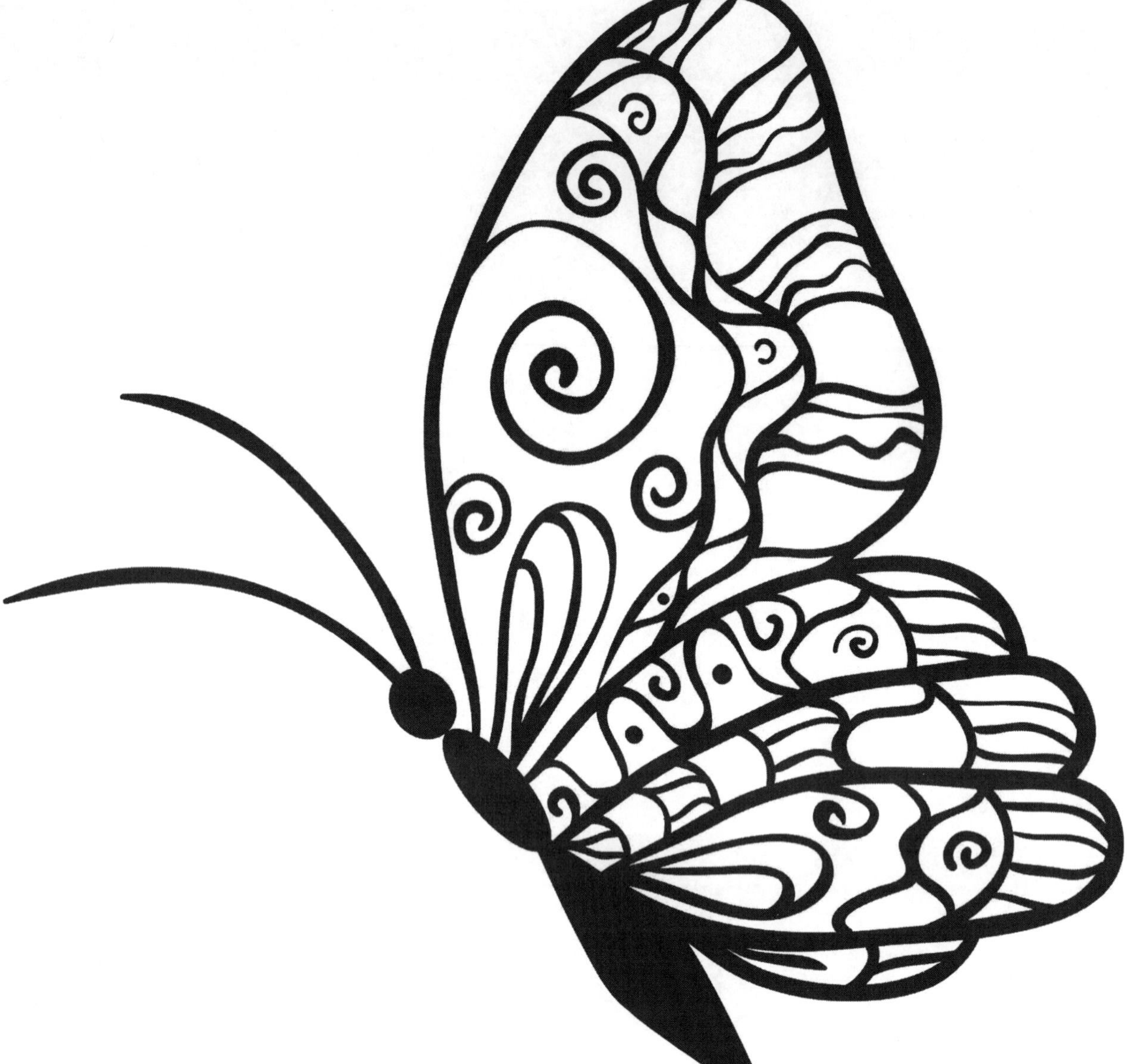

Date ....

Topic of the Day: _____

Today's Date: _____

Topic of the Day: _____

Today's Date: _____

Topic of the Day: _____
Today's Date: _____

Topic of the Day:
Today's Date:

Topic of the Day: _____
Today's Date: _____

Topic of the Day: _____
Today's Date: _____

Topic of the Day:
Today's Date:

Topic of the Day: _____

Today's Date: _____

Topic of the Day: _____
Today's Date: _____

Topic of the Day: _____

Today's Date: _____

Topic of the Day: _____
Today's Date: _____

Topic of the Day: _____

Today's Date: _____

Topic of the Day:
Today's Date:

Topic of the Day: _____
Today's Date: _____

Topic of the Day: _____
Today's Date: _____

Topic of the Day: _____
Today's Date: _____

Topic of the Day:
Today's Date:

Topic of the Day: _____

Today's Date: _____

Topic of the Day:
Today's Date:

Topic of the Day: _____

Today's Date: _____

Topic of the Day: _____
Today's Date: _____

Topic of the Day: _____
Today's Date: _____

Topic of the Day: _____
Today's Date: _____

Topic of the Day:
Today's Date:

Topic of the Day: _____
Today's Date: _____

Topic of the Day:
Today's Date:

Topic of the Day:
Today's Date:

Topic of the Day:

Today's Date:

Topic of the Day:
Today's Date:

Topic of the Day: _____

Today's Date: _____

Topic of the Day: _____

Today's Date: _____

Topic of the Day: _____

Today's Date: _____

Topic of the Day:

Today's Date:

Topic of the Day:

Today's Date:

Topic of the Day:
Today's Date:

Topic of the Day: _____
Today's Date: _____

Topic of the Day: _____
Today's Date: _____

Topic of the Day: _____
Today's Date: _____

Topic of the Day: _____
Today's Date: _____

Topic of the Day: _____

Today's Date: _____

Topic of the Day: _____
Today's Date: _____

Topic of the Day: _____

Today's Date: _____

Topic of the Day:
Today's Date:

Topic of the Day: _____

Today's Date: _____

Topic of the Day: _____

Topic of the Day:
Today's Date:

Topic of the Day: _____

Today's Date: _____

Topic of the Day:

Today's Date:

Topic of the Day: _____

Today's Date: _____

Topic of the Day: _____
Today's Date: _____

Topic of the Day: _____

Today's Date: _____

Topic of the Day:

Today's Date:

Topic of the Day:

Today's Date:

Topic of the Day: _____

Today's Date: _____

Topic of the Day:
Today's Date:

Topic of the Day: _____

Today's Date: _____

Topic of the Day: _____
Today's Date: _____

Topic of the Day: _____
Today's Date: _____

Topic of the Day: _____
Today's Date: _____

Topic of the Day: _____
Today's Date: _____

Topic of the Day: _____
Today's Date: _____

Topic of the Day: _____

Today's Date: _____

Topic of the Day: _____
Today's Date: _____

Topic of the Day:
Today's Date:

Topic of the Day: _____

Today's Date: _____

Topic of the Day: _____
Today's Date: _____

Topic of the Day:
Today's Date:

Topic of the Day: _____

Today's Date: _____

Topic of the Day:

Today's Date:

Topic of the Day: _____

Today's Date: _____

Topic of the Day:

Today's Date:

Made in the USA
Middletown, DE
06 December 2015